Leadersh

By J. J. TURNER

FORMER
INSTRUCTOR OF BIBLE AND HOMILETICS
SCHOOL OF BIBLICAL STUDIES
WEST MONROE, LA.

QUALITY PUBLICATIONS
P.O. BOX 1060
ABILENE, TEXAS 79604
(915) 677-6262

ISBN: 0-89137-123-0

Copyright 1976
By Lambert Book House, Inc.

Revised 1989
By Quality Publications

All rights reserved. No part of this publication may be reproduced, stored in a retrieval system, or transmitted in any form by any means — electronic, mechanical, photocopy, recording, or otherwise — without prior permission of the copyright owner.

About The Author

J. J. Turner has been preaching since 1964. He has served churches in Georgia, Florida, Louisiana and California. He served for 10 years as an instructor and academic dean in the School of Biblical Studies, West Monroe, La. He was founding President of Ouachita Christian Schools, and American Christian Schools of Religion. He has spoken in 40 states, 11 countries, and 6 provinces of Canada. He frequently conducts seminars on Positive Living, Leadership and Church Growth, Success-N-Marriage, Attitude Management. In February, 1987, he spoke 30 times in Germany to 4000 U. S. Army personnel on various phases of attitude management. He is a special instructor in attitude management in the Atlanta Police Academy; his poem **Atlanta's Finest** has been used worldwide in a piece of the Atlanta Police Bureau's public relation material.

Turner has written 50 books on a variety of subjects, 500 articles and 200 poems. His work has been published in 25 publications. He was the founding Editor of **Christian Family Magazine,** and **Life Builders.** He holds the M. R. E. from Alabama Christian School of Religion, the D. Min. from Luther Rice Seminary, and is a Ph. D. candidate in California Graduate School.

Table of Contents

Lesson	Page
1. Introduction To Leadership Study	7
2. Why Leaders Don't Lead	13
3. The Kind Of Leaders God Wants	19
4. Some Personal Qualities Of Leaders	26
5. Leaders Must Be Success Oriented	33
6. Some Functional Qualities Of Leadership	38
7. Leaders Must Plan	45
8. Leaders Must Set Goals	52
9. Leaders Must Evaluate	59
10. Leaders And Church Growth (I)	67
11. Leaders And Church Growth (II)	75
12. Leaders And Evangelism	83
13. Leaders And Business Meetings	94
Appendix — 125 Do's And Don'ts For Leaders	102

Preface

From David Poling's *The Last Years Of The Church* to Rich Weaver's *Let This Church Die,* the Protestant world is letting it be made known that it is in trouble. In the midst of this decline and fall of main-stream Protestantism, the neo-evangelical groups are capitalizing on the vacuum that exists within the hearts of men and women. At the same time neo-pentecostalism is drawing what little life that is left in many Protestants to their subjectivism. Thus, in the last few years there has been a renewed interest in church growth. In fact, this is the latest craze sweeping denominationalism. Every group is trying to revive and strengthen what remains as well as add to it.

In the midst of all this renewal and church growth interest, the Lord's church faces a unique opportunity and challenge. Recent polls indicate that there is a renewed interest on the part of American people in religion. Hence, we must be in the forefront of the battle for the hearts and souls of men. Add to this the command given by the Lord to the church to preach the gospel to every creature (Mark 16:15, 16), realizing that there are over four billion persons alive today, and you have no trouble in seeing why the church must get busy.

The church of today faces challenges that no other generation has faced. In order to successfully meet these challenges and lead the church to victory, the congregation of today must have bold, dynamic, trained, faithful, dedicated leadership. Such leadership, however, does not just happen or pop into existence overnight. It requires much hard work and prayer.

The purpose of this book, which is really a study in the fundamentals of leadership, is to encourage each man within the church to become a better leader. This is why, therefore, I have not directed the remarks to the elders, deacons, teachers, or any other specific group within the church. I have sought, rather, to deal with leadership in general, and hope that every man, whether he is an elder, deacon, preacher, teacher, etc., will take the lessons in this work and apply them to his present leadership situation.

I have intentionally kept the remarks brief and to the point. Leaders in today's busy world do not have time to wade through a lot of verbiage to get to the core of a subject. Do not, however, read quickly over the remarks. But, rather, think upon them and do additional study. This will insure your getting the most out of this work.

It must also be stressed that this book is designed for WORK. Each lesson has a section for discussion. Some of the lessons have evaluation forms and personal questions. Do not skip any of them. This study, therefore, will help you become a better leader if you will comply with every question and request in the lessons.

May God richly bless you as you develop your abilities for the greatest work in the world — His work.

J. J. Turner

ACKNOWLEDGMENT

I am indebted to Dr. Hollis Green for permitting this work to be one of my writing projects for the doctor of ministry degree at Luther Rice Seminary, Jacksonville, Florida.

LESSON ONE

Introduction To Leadership Study

The need for leadership within the church is critical. In a day of mass communications, rapid changes, problems, and a membership of close to three million, the church faces challenges no other generation has faced. To fulfill her mission of preaching the gospel to every creature (Mark 16:15, 16), requires dynamic, courageous, innovative leadership. Just any old haphazard approach will not get the job done; likewise, nominal, unprepared leaders will not lead the church of today (and tomorrow) to victory. If leaders are to be successful today, they must prepare, work, sacrifice, plan and give themselves totally to the task before them. Nothing less will get the job done. Challenging times demand challenging leadership.

The above mentioned leadership qualities are, as a general rule, hard to find in our day. For some reason men do not aspire to lead; neither do they seem to care for the responsibilities and headaches of leadership. Much of this can be changed with a few good challenges and good training. Many do not want any part of leadership because of the so-called leadership they have been exposed to; thus, they have a poor concept or image of leaders and their work (or lack of work). The following list illustrates some of these nominal leaders:

(1) *The figurehead leader.* This person has the "official" title of leader, but his actions and attitudes are far from it. A leader must be more than a mere "decoration" or a name on a list.

(2) *The dictator.* Webster defines a dictator as one, "considered tyrannical or oppressive." This leader delights in issuing orders and pushing everyone to follow them out. He takes authority God, nor the group, has not given him. He makes it clear that one dare not "cross" him. This type of leader really turns people off in a hurry.

(3) *The forced leader.* This kind of leader is not serving because he really wants to serve; but, rather, because pressure has been brought to bear upon him. This type will never be of much value to any congregation or leadership. A man must have a desire to be a leader.

(4) *The "they couldn't get anybody else" leader.* This type differs from the forced leader in that he is serving, not out of pressure, but out of a "need." They "need" someone to fill the

gap, or make the appropriate number, and he is coaxed into the slot. He is a "second-best" or "stop-gap" man.

(5) *The "yes man" leader.* This fellow never has an opinion, or if he does he will not express it. He never goes against the grain of popular opinion, etc. He is thoughtless and spineless! His great delight is in the fact that he is among the majority.

(6) *The mediocre leader.* This person does just enough to get by. He is unimpressive, and only desires to keep people off his back. His quality is not the best; neither is it, usually, his best. No one wants to be a part of a mediocre leadership, nor associated with such so-called leaders. Mediocrity is catching!

(7) *The pseudo dynamic leader.* To listen to this man talk, you would conclude that he is ready to "storm Jericho," or do some other great thing. But nothing ever happens. He only talks a "good fight." Talk is easy, but work is hard.

(8) *The negative leader.* No matter what the proposal may be, he is against it. His mind is closed. He can always give "101" reasons why something cannot be done instead of helping discover ways things may be done.

(9) *The financial leader.* This person has been placed in a leadership role, not because of his abilities or qualifications, but, mainly, because of his money. As long as he is permitted to "lead," he will give his money in large amounts. "Buck him" and the money will be cut down or even off. Some congregations will tolerate many things in the lives of such persons; while on the other hand, they will not tolerate similar things in the lives of the poor. "Money talks!" Even in the Lord's church.

(10) *The self-appointed leader.* Somewhere, at sometime, no one really knows how, this fellow assumed or took upon himself the responsibility of leadership. Some form their own group(s), or pull away from others, in order to have things their way. And in time, if they become outnumbered, they will "pull off" and form another group based upon the same attitude — "I WANT TO BE A LEADER!"

(11) *The "past reputation" leader.* This type may have been involved in something very dynamic in days gone by, or known for some great ability in past days; thus, based upon his past reputation he is made, without question or check, a leader in a congregation because of it. He may not be the same person or leader today as he was in the "good old days." Again, we must remember that leaders must prove themselves to the people that

INTRODUCTION TO LEADERSHIP STUDY

they are leading. A good past reputation is good, but he may not be the same man today that he was back then.

(12) *The ignorant leader*. This fellow has no idea what his responsibilities are as a leader. In some cases he will know what he is supposed to do, but because of ignorance, he cannot do it. An ignorant leader will not inspire anyone to follow him.

These, and other reasons, are why we must encourage, enlist and train men to become leaders in the church. We must not become discouraged by what has gone before, or quit because others are not doing their job. The local church, which is a group of people, will be successful in direct proportion to the effectiveness of its leadership. This is why leadership study is very, very important.

SOME DEFINITIONS

Who is a leader? And what is leadership? These questions are asked and studied frequently. The words *leader* and *leadership* convey various ideas to various persons; their understanding is based upon one's knowledge and background. This is why, therefore, there are many definitions for these two words. A sampling of these definitions will help us in developing a proper, workable, understandable attitude toward leadership. Notice for example the following definitions by Webster: *Leader:* "A person or thing that leads; directing, commanding, or guiding head, as of a group or activity;" *Leadership:* "The position or guidance of a leader; the ability to lead; the leaders of a group." To these definitions an adding of the following, which have been gleaned from many sources, will help us better define and understand these words:

(1) "Leadership is the result of one's words and actions upon another. We all influence others by our words and actions."

(2) "A leader is one who provides a method or procedure by which the group can periodically express who they desire for a leader" (Victor Durrington.)

(3) "Leadership is a process of influencing the activities of an organized group in its task of goal setting and goal achievement" (Cartwright & Zonder).

(4) "Leadership: any process by which an individual or group of individuals controls and guides the behavior of others" (Glen Posey).

(5) "Leader: . . . (finding) the ablest man . . . raise him to the supreme place, and loyally reverence him . . . what he tells

us to do must be precisely the wisest, fittest, that we could anywhere or anyhow learn . . ." (Thomas Carlyle).

(6) "Leadership is defined as the process of arranging a situation so that various members of the group, including the leader, can achieve common goals with maximum economy and a minimum of time and work" (Bellows).

(7) "Leadership is the knack of getting other people to follow you and do willingly the things you want them to do" (Lester R. Bittel).

(8) "A leader is an inspirer of others."

(9) "A leader is a person who also knows how to follow."

(10) "Leadership is giving proper direction and help so that others may become leaders, too."

(11) "Christian leadership is the prayerful and skillful activity of motivating people to achieve beneficial objectives expediently through compatible cooperation" (W. H. Souther).

(12) "Leadership is when people are going around one corner the leader is going around the next one" (Gen. T. L. Campbell).

ACROSTICALLY DEFINED

L — oyal
E — arnest
A — ctive
D — edicated
E — nthusiastic
R — espected

L — eads the way
E — fficient in work
A — vailable for service
D — elegates to others
E — xpects great things
R — eady for the unexpected
S — hows ways and means
H — elps others to victory
I — nvolved in moving forward
P — lans and prays for victory

Truly, leadership and serving as a leader, is a many faceted work that requires much prayer, training and hard work, as can be seen from the above definitions. We must never forget, however, that leadership is much, much more than qualities given by a few definitions. Definitions should inspire us toward developing our total abilities for the Lord's service.

WHY WE NEED LEADERSHIP

No institution, group, company, nation, or church will go very far without good leadership. In fact, they will never go any farther than their leaders lead them. Your congregation is at its present position and condition because of its present leadership. We need leadership, therefore, because:

(1) *There has been a lack of good, dependable leadership in*

many congregations. This is evidenced by the fact that many congregations are failing to fulfill their mission in the world.

(2) *God commanded it.* In both the Old and New Testaments we see God's wisdom issuing commands for leaders. In Exodus 18:21-23, a section we will study in some detail later, Jethro gives Moses guidelines for selecting leaders. In I Timothy 3:1-13 Paul gives the qualifications for elders and deacons. God wants leaders for His people.

(3) *Progress depends upon it.* If the church is to fulfill her task of preaching the gospel, edifying herself and doing good unto all men, it must have leadership. Progress demands it.

(4) *The world is lost.* At this moment the world's population is over four billion. This means that the church has a mission of calling four billion souls out of darkness into the kingdom of light (Col. 1:11-13; I John 5:19). This mission will not be accomplished by chance or haphazard methods. It will be accomplished to the degree of effort being put forth by leaders.

(5) *The church needs edification.* Paul wrote, "And he gave some apostles; some, prophets; and some evangelists, and some, pastors and teachers, for the perfecting of the saints, for the work of the ministry, for the edifying of the body of Christ" (Ephesians 4:11, 13).

(6) *People need it.* Poor leadership leads to trouble. Jesus cautioned, "Let them alone: they be blind leaders of the blind. And if the blind lead the blind, both shall fall into the ditch" (Matthew 15:14). The church must have leaders with clear vision.

(7) *Poor leadership hinders,* destroys and discourages the followers from reaching their greatest potential.

(8) *It inspires others.* Good leadership brings out the best in others. It motivates them to do their best.

(9) *It influences others.* Everyone is influenced by one thing or another; it's human nature. Good leadership is a positive influence in the lives of people for good.

(10) *People have problems.* It will take loving, sensitive leaders to minister to the many needs of the people. An unqualified leader will do more harm than good.

(11) *Truth must be defended.* For example, elders are commanded to hold "fast the faithful word as he hath been taught, that he may be able by sound doctrine both to exhort and to convince the gainsayers" (Titus 1:9). All Christians must defend the faith (Jude 3; I Peter 3:15).

(12) *The power of example is important.* Paul told Timothy

to be an example (I Timothy 4:12); likewise, elders must be examples to the flock (I Peter 1:3). People need to see Christ-likeness in their leaders. They need a "pattern".

(13) *Church growth depends upon leadership.* The size or lack of size will be in direct proportion to the leadership's work and planning.

(14) *Spiritual growth depends upon leadership.*

(15) *Discipline depends upon leadership.* A congregation with a weak or poor leadership will fail to purge the church of sin and mark the disorderly.

CONCLUSION

This lesson should have impressed upon your mind the tremendous need for good, dedicated leadership within the Lord's church. We will accomplish the mission assigned to us by the Lord, when we have leaders that will lead. May God help each of us to pledge ourselves to being the very best we possibly can be for the Lord's sake (I Corinthians 15:58).

FOR DISCUSSION

1. How many classes have you had in leadership training?
2. What did you get out of your last leadership class?
3. What hinders men from wanting to become leaders?
4. Who should encourage men to become leaders?
5. Should we start training our young boys in leadership? Why?
6. Why does the church need good leadership?
7. Why do some men reject responsibilities?
8. Why do leaders have headaches?
9. What is a nominal leader?
10. Discuss each nominal class mentioned in the lesson.
11. Do you agree that all are poor types of leaders?
12. List any other nominal types you may know of for discussion.
13. Why are definitions limited?
14. In what sense are definitions limited?
15. Bring your own definition of leadership to class. Discuss.
16. List additional reasons why we need to have a clear concept of leadership.
17. Discuss the reasons why we need good leadership.
18. What kind of leader are you? (Personally answer this.)
19. Do you want to improve your leadership ability?
    Yes ☐   No ☐
20. Will you work hard to improve your leadership ability?
    Yes ☐   No ☐

LESSON TWO

Why Leaders Don't Lead

"Followers will never go any further than their leaders."
"A leader is an ordinary person with extraordinary determination."
"A leader who doesn't lead is a contradiction."

INTRODUCTION

During a seminar on leadership a man asked the director this question, "Why don't leaders lead?" To this question the director replied, "That's a challenging question." As he proceeded to list reasons, my mind leaped into gear and thought of the question's application to the church: "Why don't leaders in the church lead?" Or more correctly, "Why is it that some leaders don't lead?" As I sat taking notes, as well as jotting down my own thoughts, the following answers emerged in answer to the question. Leaders don't lead because:

(1) *They lack ability.* In I Corinthians 12:13-27 the apostle Paul points out that each member of the body (church) has a different function. Leadership is a function which requires ability. Many leaders, therefore, lack ability because they do not have the inherent capacity for becoming a proficient leader. Others lack ability because they will not apply themselves to developing their inherent capacities. Potential is not synonymous with ability; neither is experience synonymous with ability. Without ability leaders don't lead. This is why, for example, deacons must first "be proven" (I Timothy 3:10).

(2) *They lack courage.* No leader has ever pleased everyone. But many leaders think they must. A leader would do well to learn early that disapproval is one of the headaches of leadership. Many leaders with great ability fail to lead because they fear what others may think, or because they fear receiving their disapproval. This leads them to hesitation in decision making; they fear the pains, rejection, or reaction from their followers. They need not feel alone, because the great leaders throughout history, e.g., Moses, Joshua, Paul, Christ, and others, did not receive everyone's approval, but because of courage and dedication they were victorious. It has rightly been said, "A man who wants to lead the orchestra must turn his back on the crowd." This is what a leader must do, he must *"turn his back"* on the few objectors, and if right, make his decision and stand by it.

(3) *They are too busy.* No matter how much ability and courage a leader has, if he doesn't have time for the responsibilities and functions of leadership, he cannot lead. A leader has time to do his job, and do it well. As the proverb states, "A person does the things he really wants to do, but complains about not having time to do the things he pretends he wants to do." Well-arranged time, therefore, is a sure mark of a well-arranged mind, (which is essential to good leadership).

(4) *Their work and responsibility is ambiguous.* Nothing is more frustrating to a leader than ambiguity relative to his leadership role. The group he is serving does not know, or has not defined his role. Some groups are not even clear as to who their leaders are, or which leader has a given responsibility. Such attitudes discourage many good leaders from becoming involved; some quickly resign under such conditions. Leaders and followers need to have clearly defined purposes if leaders are to lead effectively. In the case of elders the Bible clearly defines their work and responsibilities. Thus, Bible study is required in this case.

(5) *They are novices.* A novice, according to Webster, "is one new to any activity; a beginner." In the realm of leadership he lacks experience. He may have leadership ability, but is not able to function in certain capacities because he does not have prior experience. It is true that experience comes with time and effort, and those without experience can be trained. But it is, also, obvious that many tasks are of such magnitude that a novice

cannot handle them. In time he may, but not at first. This is why an elder must not be a novice (I Timothy 3:6). A new leader should be carefully integrated into responsibilities.

(6) *They are lazy.* This is just the opposite of being too busy. Many in the position of leadership with time and ability fail to lead because they are lazy. They lack the enthusiasm and initiative for their job. Even if a leader is on the right track, he will get run over if he just sits there. The wise man of old aptly describes the lazy man in these words, "The slothful man saith, There is a lion in the way; a lion is in the streets. As the door turneth upon its hinges, so doth the slothful upon his bed. The slothful hideth his hand in his bosom; it grieveth him to bring it again to his mouth" (Proverbs 26:13-15). It has been stated that "an indolent man is just a dead one who can't be legally buried." Thus, "While some are standing on the promises, others just sit on the premises."

(7) *They are not respected.* A leader is fighting an uphill battle trying to lead people that do not respect him. People will resent and resist a leader who (a) has questionable life habits, (b) tries to rule with an "iron fist," (c) or is never considerate of the needs and wants of the followers. Respect must not be confused with "liking or disliking" of a decision. A good leader is followed and respected even though his decisions from time to time may be frowned upon or be unpopular. Respect is an important key in leading people.

(8) *They are indecisive.* The making of decisions is a major part of being a leader. An indecisive leader only hinders progress. Whether one will admit it or not, indecision is really a decision, a decision to procrastinate. John Foster has adequately stated the true nature of indecision. He said, "Nothing can be more destructive to vigor of action than protracted, anxious, fluctuation, through resolutions adopted, rejected, resumed, and suspended, and nothing causes a greater expense of feeling. — A man without decision can never be said to belong to himself; he is as a wave of the sea, or a feather in the air which every breeze blows about as it listeth." This is not to say that there isn't a valid place for investigating and taking time in making decisions. Jesus said, "Count the cost." The perpetual habit, however, of indecision is a barrier to great leadership.

(9) *They don't know where they are going.* In the proverbial sense they "are running in circles." They don't know what to do or where to go next. They have no direction. "You cannot lead where you do not go." Perhaps you have heard the old story of the man who was running as quickly as possible after a group of people. While trying to catch up with them, he was asked the reason for his hurry. His answer was: "I've got to catch up with them. I'm their leader!" This is not leadership.

(10) *They have mixed allegiance.* They find it difficult to be totally committed to the task before them. Sometimes they have a hard time going along with the plans approved by the majority of the group. Thus they are "lukewarm" toward the effort. A few, sad to say, may even be wrestling with their dedication to the cause of Christ. God wants our allegiance every hour in the day, and every day in the week, and every week in the year.

(11) *They procrastinate.* These kind of leaders are always putting off until tomorrow what they should do today. Cliff Cole has rightly said, "Procrastination is not only the thief of time but it clutters up our lives with an appalling number of half-done things and with slovenly habits." Thus, the leader who waits to do a great deal at once will never do anything. Life and leadership is made up of little things. Today is the day of ACTION!

(12) *They are pessimistic.* This quality must not be confused with a lack of courage. Pessimism is just plain old negative thinking. Its favorite expression is, "It can't be done." It has been said that a pessimist is someone "who likes to listen to the patter of little defeats." Thus, the pessimistic leader who says that it cannot be done is likely to be interrupted by someone doing it.

(13) *They lack tact.* It seems that everytime this type opens his mouth he is offending someone or hurting their feelings. A good leader must make his point without making an enemy; especially, because of his attitude. Someone has left us the following tact formula: "Be brief, politely; be aggressive, smilingly; be emphatic, pleasantly; be positive, diplomatically; be right, graciously." There is a right and wrong way to approach every person or situation. Leaders must, therefore, pray for wisdom to make the right approach.

(14) *They walk by sight.* The real leader walks by faith (II Corinthians 5:7). He believes that with God's help all things are possible. In contrast the leader who walks by sight never has a faith larger than the balance on the check book. His favorite question is, "How much will it cost?" If every aspect of the suggested project is not financially covered or within easy reach, he advocates waiting for the time when "WE" can do it without help. No one is encouraged by such leadership to launch out by faith and trust God to provide.

(15) *They are content with remaining status quo.* This spirit is content to remain in the same rut or position of accomplishment. Such leaders are content to do the same things in the same way, year after year. This does not mean that these things are wrong. It rather implies, however, that progress may be halted, and followers discouraged, because of no vision, planning or desire to do even greater things in the Lord's service. "Don't rock the boat," is the motto of such leaders.

CONCLUSION

What is the solution to these problems within a leadership? What should be done if these problems exist within a congregation? The following suggestions are possible solutions:

(1) Pray for wisdom to handle them properly (James 1:2-6).

(2) Discuss the problem.

(3) Ask unqualified to step down if they are not willing to change. (This will take time, patience, and tact.)

(4) Enlist and train leaders.

(5) Appoint those already qualified.

(6) Be sure that each position is clearly defined.

(7) Support your leaders.

(8) Keep channels of communications open.

(9) Urge all to count the cost before accepting the responsibility.

(10) Always try to upgrade your own proficiency.

FOR DISCUSSION

1. Discuss the quotations under the chapter title.
2. List any other reasons you have relative to why leaders don't lead.
3. How would one leader, like discussed in this lesson, affect the rest of the leaders?
4. Are leaders "born" leaders? Discuss.
5. What is the source of a person's ability?
6. How can one know if he has leadership ability?
7. Why is courage important? Give an example of a leader with courage.
8. What should a man do if he is too busy to lead?
9. Why should a leader know clearly what his job is?
10. How does a novice gain experience?
11. What makes a person lazy? What is the best cure for laziness?
12. How is the best way to gain respect? How is respect lost?
13. Why is indecision harmful? What makes a person indecisive?
14. How far should a leader go by faith? How far by sight?
15. Why is status quo so popular?
16. How should leadership problems be discussed? When? Where?
17. Why is it difficult to ask an unqualified person to step down? How is the best way to approach this problem?
18. Why should a leader count the cost? Did you? Will you?
19. How is the best way to train leaders?
20. How can leadership be constantly upgraded?
21. What have you learned from this lesson that will help you to be a better leader? What do you plan to do with the facts learned in this chapter?
22. Discuss a good example of tact and a poor example of tact.
23. What causes a person to be pessimistic?
24. Why do leaders keep putting things off?
25. Why do some leaders fail to know where they are going?

LESSON THREE

The Kind Of Leaders God Wants

INTRODUCTION

It is a well-known truth in business circles that companies rise and fall according to their leadership. Millions of dollars are spent each year by businesses to train their leaders. They know from experience that a company will not go forward without dynamic, dedicated leadership. Someone has rightly said, "Every institution is but the lengthened shadow of its leaders." The church is no exception.

The leadership truths so relevant to business and success are also relevant and needful in the Lord's church today. It is hard, also, for a congregation to go forward without a dynamic, faithful leadership. For too long in some congregations, we have sought for volunteers and the "born leaders" to do the job of leading the local congregation. We have done this to the exclusion of training and preparing men to take a part in the ongoing of the local church. As usual, we have waited until the world has proven that leaders are "made" and not "born". It has been encouraging, however, in recent years to see the emphasis increase toward leadership training within many local congregations.

OLD TESTAMENT EXAMPLE

Contrary to what some seem to think, leadership is ordained of God. Moses, for example, always comes to mind when great leaders are considered. Many do not realize, however, that Moses needed special help and instruction in the task of leadership. In the Old Testament, therefore, leadership is exemplified.

In Exodus chapter 18 we read the account of Moses wearing himself out trying to provide leadership and guidance for the people of Israel. Finally his father-in-law, Jethro, comes upon the scene and gives him some sage advice relative to his working with the people as a leader. A reading of verses 21 and 22 will reveal the kind of leaders needed in Moses' situation. Notice the six qualities Moses was to look for as he selected men to aid him in the task of leadership. He was told to select (1) able men, (2) men that feared God, (3) men of truth, (4) men who hate covetousness, (5) men that could delegate authority and jobs, and (6) men who were available. It is obvious that God still desires these same qualities today in the lives of the men who lead in His service. Let us notice these six qualities for a moment.

First, a leader must be an able man. What could be worse than having a man trying to do a job that he is not able to do? Webster defines able as, "having enough power, skill, etc. to do something." Obviously then, not just anybody will do in the position of leadership among God's people. Paul wrote concerning elders, "If a man knoweth not how to rule his own house, how shall he rule the church of God?" (I Tim. 3:5). In admonishing Timothy, Paul encouraged him to train men "who shall be able to teach others also" (II Tim. 2:2). How does a man become able? Through desire, prayer and preparation. God still needs ABLE men.

Second, a leader must fear God. No doubt the fear under consideration in our text is reverence and holy respect for God. Where there is a lack of reverence for God, destruction and failure are the sure products (Rom. 2:10-18). The Wise Man said, "This is the end of the matter, all hath been heard; fear God, and keep his commandments, for this is the whole duty of man" (Eccl. 12:13). A reverent leader will inspire others to love God and follow the Lord's will in church work.

Third, a leader is a man of truth. This is in harmony with Christ's statement about the efficacy of the truth (Jno. 8:32). A leader must not only be a man of truth, he must also know the truth, teach the truth, and stand for the truth at all cost. He will study diligently for it, and not "sell" it at any price (Prov. 23:23). If the leaders do not know the truth, then the followers may be led into a ditch (Matt. 15:14).

Fourth, a leader must hate covetousness. To do so will assure its absence from the hearts of those who follow, as well as insisting that it be removed from the hearts of those who are troubled with it. This greedy, lustful condition is constantly condemned throughout the Bible (Cf. II Pet. 2:16; Rom. 1:29; Eph. 5:3; I Thess. 3:3), and is at the bottom of every sin committed.

Fifth, a leader delegates authority and work. This was one of Moses' problems: he tried to do it all by himself. No man, no matter how strong or talented, can do it all alone. A good leader inspires and encourages others to share in the work and responsibilities. This will free him to do additional tasks, etc. Once a leader has delegated a job and the authority and means to back it up, he does not constantly "peep" around the corner, worrying if the job will get done: he trusts his delegates because he has prepared them for the task.

Sixth, a leader is available. He knows that leadership is not just an "executive" position where commands are arbitrarily issued with no personal contact, involvement or concern for possible problems and needs which may arise. The leader is never "to busy" to give personal help and counsel in time of need. He is ready, willing and able to help a brother finish a task in the Lord's service.

It is obvious, then, that there is no place within God's economy for (1) a figurehead leader, (2) a dictatorial leader, (3) a wishy-washy leader, (4) a mediocre leader, (5) a "name only" leader, or (6) a "drafted" leader. God still wants His leaders to have the same qualities as described in our text (Rom. 15:4.) May God help us to prepare ourselves, and others, for the great task of leadership in the greatest service in the world — God's service.

NEW TESTAMENT EXAMPLES

When we come to the New Testament we see many examples of leadership. The following points continue the exemplification of the kind of leaders God wants, and the kind he uses:

The Apostles are examples of leaders approved by God. A survey of their lives and the facts revealed about them will reveal the following facts:

(1) They were from different backgrounds, e.g., tax collector, fisherman, religious leaders, etc. God uses leaders today with different backgrounds.

(2) When called to follow Jesus, these men were busy. The Lord did not call any inactive persons to follow Him. He placed active men into new roles. Today, God uses active men.

(3) These men had the desire to serve. They left all to follow Jesus "straight way". No one forced them to serve. This is needful in the leaders of today. They must have a desire to lead.

(4) These men received training. For some three to three and a half years they were personally taught and trained by Jesus. Men, obviously, must be taught and trained today for the work of leadership.

(5) These men were obedient to the Master. They followed the Lord's instructions, e.g., Acts 1 and 2.

(6) These men chose replacements when needed (Cf. Acts 1:15-26). Leaders still need to prepare men to succeed them. Everyone will one day need replacing.

(7) These men were bold, faithful and uncompromising (Cf. Acts 4, etc.).

(8) These men finished the task assigned them. They were not quitters. We, too, must finish the task assigned us by the Lord.

(9) These men lead the way.

(10) These men were examples. God still needs these qualities today!

The seven are examples of leaders selected by God. This account of selecting deacons is recorded in Acts 6. The directive was, "look ye out among you seven men of honest report, full of the Holy Spirit and wisdom, whom ye may appoint over this business" (verse 3). From this account it is obvious God wants leaders who are:

(1) Reported to be good men. This requires background information.

(2) Willing to serve — "may appoint". (Again, He never forces).

(3) Wise men. God gives wisdom to those who ask (James 1:5).

(4) Full of the Holy Spirit, i.e., today "Fruits of the Spirit" (Gal. 5:22-26).

(5) Dependable men — "over this business." (They could handle it.)

(6) Able men. (This is an obvious point).

THE KIND OF LEADERS GOD WANTS

In I Timothy 3:8-13 we have the qualifications for a deacon. While it is not within the scope of this work to study the qualifications and works of elders and deacons, it will be necessary, however, for these to be studied before men are appointed to these offices.

Elders are examples of leaders. According to God's word these men have the oversight of local congregations (Acts 20:28; I Peter 5:1-5). A survey of the Scriptures will reveal their work and qualifications. By way of quick review notice their qualifications as set forth by the apostle Paul in I Timothy 3:1-7.

(1) A man must desire the office (3:1).
(2) He desires a work.
(3) He must be blameless.
(4) The husband of one wife.
(5) Vigilant.
(6) Sober.
(7) Good behavior.
(8) Given to hospitality.
(9) Apt to teach.
(10) Not given to wine.
(11) No striker.
(12) Not greedy of filthy lucre.
(13) Patient.
(14) Not a brawler.
(15) Not covetous.
(16) Ruleth own house well.
(17) Children in subjection.
(18) Not a novice.
(19) Have a good report from without.

As stated before, it is essential that the work and qualifications of elders be studied in detail. Our point is, many of the above qualities are expected in ALL leaders and Christians.

Evangelists are examples of leaders. Sad to say, in many congregations, if any leading gets done, the preacher does it. This is not so much a reflection upon him as it is on the members of the congregation who will not prepare themselves to accept leadership responsibilities. The Bible presents a number of qualities that the evangelists should possess if he is to be a leader approved unto God. Some of these are as follows:

(1) He must be a pure man (I Timothy 4:12; 5:22).
(2) He must be an example in life style, etc. (I Timothy 4:12).
(3) He must be a man of faith, love, righteousness, patience, meekness, etc. (I Timothy 6:11; II Timothy 2:22).
(4) He must be a student of the Bible (II Timothy 2:15).
(5) He must be able to teach and train others (II Timothy 2:2).
(6) He must avoid foolish and ignorant questions (II Timothy 2:16, 23; Titus 3:9, 10).
(7) He must be willing to suffer hardship as a good soldier (II Timothy 2:3; 4:5).
(8) He must preach the word (II Timothy 4:1-5).
(9) He must set in order the things that are lacking (Titus 1:5).
(10) He ordains elders (Titus 1:5).
(11) He is an example (I Timothy 4:12).
(12) He is not ashamed of the testimony of the Lord (II Timothy 1:8).
(13) He works to fulfill his duties (I Timothy 4:15, 16; II Timothy 4:5).
(14) He loves lost souls (Acts 8:29-40).
(15) He defends the faith (truth) (I Timothy 1:18, 19; I Peter 3:15; Jude 3).

The local congregation will grow and glow when the evangelist is doing his work as God prescribed. (Of course this is a general rule. Some preachers are hindered from doing their work.)

CONCLUSION

Every business, government, institution, etc., has its qualifications and ideals for its leaders. Therefore, we should not be surprised to learn that God has always made known the kind of leaders He wants to lead His people. A listing of all the above attributes, from both Testaments, will give a clear picture of the kind of leaders God wants. To this list we may add many others, but we must be careful not to take any away. Let's have the kind of leaders God wants! Make up your mind that you are going to be the kind of leader God wants. Do it now!

THE KIND OF LEADERS GOD WANTS

FOR DISCUSSION

1. Why does success depend upon leadership?
2. Why should the church be interested in leadership success?
3. Discuss the statement, "Every institution is but the lengthened shadow of it leaders."
4. Why did God ordain leadership?
5. Why is an Old Testament example important to our study of leadership?
6. Can you name any other Old Testament accounts of leadership? Discuss some.
7. Why did Moses need help?
8. Where did Jethro get his leadership information?
9. Why, in both Testaments, do we find the Lord always wanting ABLE men?
10. Why is reverence important?
11. Why should leaders delegate authority?
12. Discuss some of the leadership qualities of the apostles.
13. What kind of leader was Peter?
14. Can you point out any poor qualities in any of the apostles? Were they corrected?
15. Briefly discuss the work of deacons.
16. Have you studied the work and qualifications of elders? When?
17. Should all Christians possess the qualities of an elder? Which one(s) may be the exception?
18. Why do most preachers end up leading the congregation?
19. Have you ever studied the work and qualifications of an evangelist?
20. Can you list any other qualifications of an evangelist?
21. List the qualities from the above study that appear more than once in the listings.
22. Do you want to be the kind of leader God wants? Do you want the kind God wants?

LESSON FOUR

Some Personal Qualities Of Leaders

INTRODUCTION

In the last lesson we noted some of the qualities God wants in His leaders. In this lesson we want to notice some additional qualities that must be characteristic of leaders. These qualities will assist them in becoming the kind of leaders people will proudly follow. This lesson will differ in approach because questions will be listed after each quality for your personal response. Thus, there will be no questions at the end for discussion. Each point, however, should be discussed in class.

20 PERSONAL QUALITIES OF LEADERS

1. *Leaders are persons of ability.*
    a. "Every person is responsible for all the good within the scope of his abilities, and for no more, and none can tell whose sphere is the largest" (Hamilton).
    b. "The question "Who ought to be boss?" is like asking "Who ought to be the tenor in the quartet?" Obviously, "the man who can sing tenor" (Henry Ford).
    c. "Moreover, thou shalt provide out of all the people able men . . . and place them over them . . ." (Exodus 18:21).
    d. I believe I have leadership ability. ☐ Yes ☐ No
    I want to find out if I have ability. ☐ Yes ☐ No
    I want to develop leadership ability. ☐ Yes ☐ No

2. *Leaders are persons of belief.*
    a. "In belief lies the secret of all valuable exertion" (Bulwer).
    b. "Remember that what you believe will depend very much upon what you are" (Noah Porter).

— 26 —

SOME PERSONAL QUALITIES OF LEADERS

    c. "All things are possible to him that believeth . . ." (Mark 9:23).
    d. Do you believe in the cause of Christ, totally? ☐ Yes ☐ No
       Do you believe in yourself? ☐ Yes ☐ No
       Do you believe in others? ☐ Yes ☐ No

3. *Leaders must have courage.*
    a. "Courage consists, not in blindly overlooking danger, but in seeing and conquering it" (Richter).
    b. "Courage is, on all hands, considered as an essential of high character" (Froude).
    c. ". . . be ye of good courage" (Numbers 13:20).
    d. Do you have courage to lead? ☐ Yes ☐ No
    will you help others to be courageous? ☐ Yes ☐ No

4. *Leaders must be diligent.*
    a. "He who labors diligently need never despair; for all things are accomplished by diligence and labor" (Menander).
    b. "The expectations of life depend upon diligence" (Confucius).
    c. "The hand of the diligent shall bear rule . . ." (Proverbs 12:24).
    d. Do you consider yourself a diligent person? ☐ Yes ☐ No
    Do you approach the Lord's work with diligence? ☐ Yes ☐ No

5. *Leaders are men of enthusiasm.*
    a. "Every great and commanding movement in the annals of the world is the triumph of enthusiasm . . . nothing great was ever achieved without it" (Emerson).
    b. "Every production of genius must be the production of enthusiasm" (Disraeli).
    c. "Who gave himself for us, that he might redeem us from all iniquity, and purify unto himself a peculiar people, ZEALOUS of good works" (Titus 2:14).
    d. Do you consider yourself an enthusiastic person? ☐ Yes ☐ No
    Do you have enthusiasm for the Lord's work? ☐ Yes ☐ No
    Will you try to be more enthusiastic day by day? ☐ Yes ☐ No

6. *Leaders are friendly persons.*
   a. "He alone has lost the art to live who cannot win new friends" (Weir Mitchell).
   b. "Let me live in a house by the side of the road and be a friend to man" (Sam Walter Foss).
   c. "A man that hath friends must shew himself friendly: and there is a friend that sticketh closer than a brother" (Proverbs 18:24).
   d. Do you consider yourself a friendly person?
      ☐ Yes ☐ No
      Will you try to make a new friend today?
      ☐ Yes ☐ No
      Do you make friends easily? ☐ Yes ☐ No

7. *Leaders must have goals.*
   a. "A man without a goal is like a ship without a rudder."
   b. "There must be a goal before you can reach it."
   c. "I press toward the mark for the prize of the high calling of God in Christ Jesus" (Phil. 3:14).
   d. Do you have personal goals? ☐ Yes ☐ No
      Do you know how to set goals for your personal life?
      ☐ Yes ☐ No
      Will you pledge yourself to become a better goal setter and reacher from now on? ☐ Yes ☐ No

8. *Leaders must be honest.*
   a. "Honesty is the best policy" (Franklin).
   b. "To be honest, as the world goes, is to be one man picked out of a thousand" (Shakespeare).
   c. "Provide things honest in the sight of all men" (Romans 12:17).
   d. Do you practice honesty in all areas of your life?
      ☐ Yes ☐ No
      Do others consider you an honest person?
      ☐ Yes ☐ No
      Will you be honest in every area of leadership?
      ☐ Yes ☐ No

9. *Leaders must be industrious.*
   a. "If you have great talents, industry will improve them; if moderate abilities, industry will supply their deficiencies. Nothing is denied to well-directed labor; nothing is ever to be attained without it" (Sir Joshua Reynolds).

SOME PERSONAL QUALITIES OF LEADERS

    b. "A lack of activity will insure more inactivity."
    c. "Whatsoever thy hands find to do, do it with all thine might" (Eccl. 9:10).
    d. Are you an industrious leader? ☐ Yes ☐ No
Do you plan to work harder than ever before for the cause of Christ? ☐ Yes ☐ No

10. *Leaders are persons of justice.*
    a. "Justice is the great and simple principle which is the secret of success in all government, as essential to the training of an infant, as to the control of a mighty nation" (Simms).
    b. "Justice discards party, friendship, and kindred, and is therefore represented as blind" (Addison).
    c. "He hath showed thee O man, what is good; and what doth the Lord require of thee, but to do justly, and to love mercy, and walk humbly with thy God" (Micah 6:8).
    d. Do you believe in justice for all? ☐ Yes ☐ No
Do you consider yourself a just person under all circumstances? ☐ Yes ☐ No

11. *Leaders are knowledgeable persons.*
    a. "Knowledge is the eye of desire and can become the pilot of the soul" (Will Durant).
    b. "Accurate knowledge is the basis of correct opinions; the want of it makes the opinions of most people of little value" (C. Simmons).
    c. "And beside this, give diligence, add to your faith virtue; and to virtue KNOWLEDGE" (II Peter 1:5).
    d. Do you study to increase your knowledge? ☐ Yes ☐ No
Do you feel knowledgeable as a leader? ☐ Yes ☐ No
Will you work to increase your knowledge for leadership purposes? ☐ Yes ☐ No

12. *Leaders must LEAD.*
    a. "Followers will never go any further than their leaders."
    b. "A leader sees three things: what ought to be done, what can be done, and how to do it."
    c. "I lead in the way of righteousness, in the midst of the paths of judgment" (Proverbs 8:20).
    d. Do you consider yourself a leader? ☐ Yes ☐ No
Do you know where you are going? ☐ Yes ☐ No
Should people follow where you lead? ☐ Yes ☐ No

13. *Leaders are mature men.*
    a. "Maturity is the ability to live in someone else's world" (Oren Arnold).
    b. "A mature person is too big to be little."
    c. "And ye are complete (mature, jjt) in him, which is the head of all principality and power" (Col. 2:10).
    d. Do you have maturity in leadership ability?
    ☐ Yes   ☐ No
    Do you know what spiritual maturity is?
    ☐ Yes   ☐ No
14. *Leaders are noble persons.*
    a. "It is better to be nobly remembered, than nobly born" (Ruskin).
    b. "The best school of nobility is the imitation of Christ" (F. D. Huntington).
    c. "Therefore, if any man be in Christ, he is a new creature: old things are passed away, behold, all things are become new" (II Cor. 5:17).
    d. Do you see yourself as a noble person? ☐ Yes   ☐ No
15. *Leaders are optimists.*
    a. "Optimism is one of the chief members of the faith family."
    b. "An optimist has been defined as "one who makes the best of it when he gets the worst of it."
    c. "I can do all things through Christ, which strengtheneth me" (Phil. 4:13).
    d. Are you an optimist?   ☐ Yes   ☐ No
    Do you fully understand the value of optimism?
    ☐ Yes   ☐ No
16. *Leaders are prayerful.*
    a. "Practice in life whatever you pray for, and God will give it to you more abundantly" (Pusey).
    b. "The greater thy business is, by so much more thou hast need to pray for God's good-speed and blessings upon it . . . therefore, though thy haste be never so much, or thy business never so great, yet go not about it, nor out of thy doors, till thou hast prayed" (James R. Bayley).
    c. "And he (Jesus, jjt) spake a parable unto them to this end, that men ought always to pray, and not to faint" (Luke 18:1). "Pray without ceasing" (I Thess. 5:17).

SOME PERSONAL QUALITIES OF LEADERS 31

    d. Do you believe in the power of prayer? ☐ Yes   ☐ No
       Should leaders be great men of prayer? ☐ Yes   ☐ No
       Will you work harder on your prayer life?
                                                  ☐ Yes   ☐ No

17. *A leader realizes the value of quietness.*
    a. "What sweet delight a quiet life affords" (Drummand).
    b. "In time of quietness our hearts should be like trees, lifting their branches to the sky to draw down strength which they will need to face the storms that will surely come" (Toyohiko Kagawa).
    c. "But we beseech you . . . study to be quiet" (I Thess. 4:10, 11); "Be still . . ." (Psalm 46:10).
    d. Do you find time for a quiet period each day?
                                                ☐ Yes   ☐ No
       Do you see the value of a period of quiet time?
                                                ☐ Yes   ☐ No

18. *Leaders must be reliable.*
    a. "Reliability is more important than ability; tackle-ability is really more to be commended than capability."
    b. "A reliable man will never be libelous."
    c. "Moreover it is required in stewards, that a man be found faithful" (I Cor. 4:2).
    d. Do you consider yourself a reliable person?
                                                ☐ Yes   ☐ No
       Do others consider you reliable?   ☐ Yes   ☐ No

19. *A leader must stand.*
    a. "When pulling together means pulling away from God, a Christian (leader, jjt) must be willing to stand alone" (Margaret Troutt).
    b. "To stand when others have run, takes integrity and courage."
    c. "Stand fast in the faith . . ." (I Cor. 16:13); "Having done all . . . stand" (Eph. 6:13).
    d. As a leader are you willing to take a stand for the truth?
                                                ☐ Yes   ☐ No
       Will you pray for courage to be able to take a stand?
                                                ☐ Yes   ☐ No

20. *Leaders must think.*
    a. "When everyone thinks alike, few are doing much thinking" (Nashua Cavalier).

b. "What a person thinks greatly determines what he becomes."
c. "Thought begets the will to create" (Thomas J. Watson).
d. "As a man thinketh in his heart, so is he" (Prov. 23:7).
e. Do you like to think for yourself? ☐ Yes ☐ No
   Do you consider yourself a deep thinker?
   ☐ Yes ☐ No
   Will you work on improving your thinking?
   ☐ Yes ☐ No

CONCLUSION
Qualities of a Good Leader

A leader is . . .
   Slow to suspect — quick to trust,
   Slow to condemn — quick to justify,
   Slow to offend — quick to defend,
   Slow to expose — quick to shield,
   Slow to reprimand — quick to forbear,
   Slow to belittle — quick to appreciate,
   Slow to demand — quick to give,
   Slow to provoke — quick to help,
   Slow to resent — quick to forgive:
      . . . A leader loves. (Unknown)

10 RULES FOR LEADERS

1. A leader shall mind his own business and not gossip.
2. A leader shall not wear his feelings on his sleeves or be so sensitive that he looks for personal offenses or slights.
3. A leader shall wear a smile. When he is gloomy, he will go away and hide rather than inflict himself and others.
4. A leader shall be considerate of others.
5. A leader shall not be headstrong.
6. A leader shall play the game of life on the square.
7. A leader shall hold his temper and each night ask God to forgive him as he forgives his neighbor.
8. A leader shall face the world each morning with confidence, determined to be as happy and brave as he can.
9. A leader shall stand and work for a worthy cause.
10. A leader shall crucify his ego and depend upon God for help.

(Unknown)

LESSON FIVE
Leaders Must Be Success Oriented

INTRODUCTION

A casual look in most book stores will reveal man's great concern for success. This is evidenced by the many books written to give advice in this area. Books on how to achieve success remain among the top sellers in the self-help field. And every now and then one will make the national best seller list. Some of these books are good, and some are not so good. A few center around an ego sefishness that is contrary to biblical teaching. God's leaders will shun this philosophy in their quest for information on success.

Christian leaders must be interested in success. Webster defines *success* as, "a favorable or satisfactory outcome or result." Success, according to another definition, "is the acquiring of a predetermined goal." Success, therefore, is the product of good leadership and is well within Christian ethics. Good leaders will seek to lead others in reaching goals within God-approved bounds and methods. They are quick to reject the "success at any cost" success formula. Success that is approved by God is not the result of chance or accident. It comes through many hours of prayer, planning and hard work. The Christian leader, above all leaders, knows this and is dedicated to leading others along the road to success.

BIBLE APPROVES OF SUCCESS

It surprises many people that the Bible approves of success. For some reason, many seem to think that success is limited to the secular, or areas outside the church. Not so! From the beginning to the end, the Bible exemplifies success, especially in the lives of certain persons: for example, Jesus Christ. The Saviour came into the world to accomplish a task (reach a goal). He stated prior to His death, ". . . it is finished" (John 19:30). Jesus was a success in doing the Father's will, etc. Christ, the prime example of success, gave the early disciples the goal of preaching the gospel to every creature (Mark 16:15, 16). In Colossians 1:23, we learn that the goal was successfully met by the early church. The early church was a successful church, just as God intended.

PAUL'S SUCCESS FORMULA

Another outstanding example of success is the apostle Paul. Many refer to Paul as the most successful Christian who has ever lived. Paul was not only successful in his service to Christ, but also in his service to Judaism (Cf. Galatians 1:11-17, etc.). After his conversion he did not become a failure, but rather a greater success than ever. He drew from his success-oriented mind. He went on three missionary journeys; thirteen epistles are attributed to his pen; and he established many churches, etc. His life and writings are full of the characteristics of success. Note for example his success formula in Philippians 3:12-14:

> "Not that I have already obtained, or am already perfect: but I press on, if so be that I may lay hold on that for which also I was laid hold on by Christ Jesus. Brethren, I count not myself yet to have laid hold: But one thing I do, forgetting the things which are behind, and stretching forward to the things that are before, I press on toward the goal unto the prize of the high calling of God in Christ Jesus."

The following brief analysis of these verses will reveal some dynamic, biblical keys to success:

First, Paul acknowledged that achievement is a continual process, and does not come quickly: "Not that I have already obtained." It takes a person of deep convictions and humility to make such a statement. The church has an ever-challenging goal before her — to preach the gospel to every creature — that she must not shirk from or give up on because it seems too hard. Success requires work.

Second, Paul set goals and kept his eyes upon them. He said, ". . . this one thing I do . . ." He knew where he was going and

LEADERS MUST BE SUCCESS ORIENTED 35

how he was going to get there. He moved with passion and dedication toward his goals. We will never reach the goals we have set without this same dedication. Every success book agrees with Paul's statement about goals.

Third, he refused to dwell on the past; whether in the areas of success or failure, the past was behind. He said, "forgetting those things which are behind . . ." A good leader realizes that dwelling on past failures could be disastrous. Likewise, past success does not ensure one today. We learn from past failures and successes, but today is a new challenge.

Fourth, Paul was excited about challenges and possibilities ahead of him. He said, ". . . reaching forth to those things which are before . . ." He was enthusiastic about the future and knew that he must be willing to cope with it. All leaders love challenges and opportunities brought by a new day, etc.

Fifth, Paul, the dynamic leader, never gave up or lost his desire. He said, ". . . I press on . . ." As a leader, he was willing to work and agonize toward reaching his "mark". It is only by personal discipline and determination that worthwhile goals are achieved.

Sixth, the apostle never doubted, with God's help, that he would acquire "the prize" sought. He had the optimism of a winner; even though he was still running the race, he knew he would win.

Seventh, as a man with many tasks and desires before him, Paul never lost sight of his priority: "of the high calling of God." With his priorities in focus and God's help, he succeeded.

Before closing, I would like to note two additional passages of scripture written by Paul and add two additional qualities to his success formula (there are many others). One of these qualities is POSITIVE THINKING. Romans 8:31, Paul wrote, "If God be for us, who can be against us?" Another quality is SELF-CONFIDENCE. To the Philippians, he wrote, "I can do all things through Christ which strengtheneth me" (Phil. 4:13). In summary, Paul's success formula consists of the following nine points:
    (1) Diligent work is involved in success.
    (2) Set goals and keep your eyes upon them.
    (3) Do not dwell in the past.
    (4) Be enthusiastic about opportunities and challenges.
    (5) Never give up or lose your desire.
    (6) Never leave God out of your plans (He is the key).

(7) Keep your priorities in their proper order.
(8) Be a positive thinker.
(9) Have confidence in yourself (Christ will help).

Whether it is leadership on the job, in the church, in the community, at school, or in the home, we, too, can succeed if we use Paul's formula for success.

ADDITIONAL THOUGHTS ON SUCCESS

The following bit of information describes the attitudes of those who climb the ladder of success:

A LADDER OF SUCCESS

____ 100% I did
____ 90% I will
____ 80% I can
____ 70% I think I can
____ 60% I might
____ 50% I think I might
____ 40% What is it?
____ 30% I wish I could
____ 20% I don't know how
____ 10% I can't
____ 0% I won't

Check which rung of the success ladder you are presently on. If you are at the bottom wake up and begin your climb. Because successful is the man who goes straight forward — with an aim on only what is right. Put every rung under your foot until you reach the top. If you slip or fall, get up and keep going with God's help. The following words by Henry Van Dyke strike at the heart of the secret of success. He said, "Four things a man must learn to do if he would make his record true:

To think without confusion, clearly,
To love his fellowman sincerely;
To act from honest motives purely;
To trust in God and heaven securely."

SUCCESS ACROSTIC

S — ervice
U — nyielding to temptations
C — hrist is the center of life
C — hallenges are accepted
E — nthusiastic about work
S — teadfast in service
S — acrificial for the cause of Christ

LEADERS MUST BE SUCCESS ORIENTED

CONCLUSION

Take your Bible and see how many additional qualities you can deduct from Paul's life and add them to the list in this lesson. Also, gather as many additional thoughts as you can and add to the above thoughts on leadership. May God bless you as you seek to serve Him and lead others successfully to the goals set before us. Always remember these words of Paul, ". . . be ye steadfast, unmoveable, always abounding in the work of the Lord, forasmuch as ye know that your labour is not in vain in the Lord" (I Corinthians 15:58).

FOR DISCUSSION

1. Why is there a concern with success?
2. How does God's standard of success differ from the world's?
3. Should Christian leaders be interested in success? Why?
4. Do you consider your congregation a success? Discuss.
5. How was Jesus a success? Why was He successful?
6. What are the goals of the church?
7. Discuss the success of the early church.
8. Do externals determine success?
9. How was Paul successful before his conversion?
10. How was Paul successful after his conversion?
11. Do most persons think that success, if it is coming, will come quickly? Why?
12. Why should we have personal goals?
13. Why will dwelling in the past hinder progress?
14. Why should we be excited about the possibilities ahead?
15. What should motivate our desire for success?
16. Why is positive thinking important to success?
17. Will God help us be successful? Discuss.
18. What is self-confidence? Is it wrong? Why?
19. Discuss the various attitudes on the "ladder of success."
20. Which rung are you on? How long will you remain on it?
21. Discuss the acrostic of success. Write your own success acrostic.
22. List any other qualities of success you can think of.
23. Discuss this statement: "Success comes in cans. Failure comes in can'ts."
24. Discuss this statement: "Only in dictionaries does *success* come before *work*."

LESSON SIX
Some Functional Qualities Of Leadership

INTRODUCTION

Leadership is not an easy task. It involves many, many hours of planning and hard work. It is obvious, therefore, that leadership involves a person in a multiple of jobs and responsibilities. This is why a leader is not an "ordinary" person. He is a very versatile person. This versatility is essential for leadership success. The following functions of leadership will exemplify some of the many works and functions of leaders.

LEADERS MUST MAKE DECISIONS

The making of decisions is one of the most challenging jobs of leadership. In fact, many men reject leadership roles because they don't like to make decisions. Others reject the job because they cannot make decisions. Decision making, however, as we all know is one of the things that life is made out of. Each day we make numerous decisions, e.g., what we shall wear; the route we shall drive; how we shall act; what we shall eat; where we shall go, etc. Obviously, then, life is one long series of decisions and choices. Many of these decisions are minor and some are major with far reaching consequences. Failure is experienced in both areas. The challenge, therefore, in all decision making is to make the proper one. Leadership is concerned with making good decisions and carrying them out.

In the day to day functions of the church many decisions must be made. For the most part these are routine and can be carried out with relative ease. But from time to time, however, major decisions must be made that will determine the growth, unity, and future of the local congregation. Leaders must be prepared to face these challenges.

SOME FUNCTIONAL QUALITIES OF LEADERSHIP

It should be noted that decisions consist basically of the following variety:

(1) Routine decisions which are somewhat easy. They occur frequently and are handled with ease.

(2) Emergency decisions that arise without warning on the spur of the moment. For example the preacher may suddenly resign, or you must settle a problem among members, etc.

(3) Pressure decisions. These result from persons trying to get certain things.

(4) Decisions to change procedures, facilities, programs, routines, etc. These may be called innovations or desired changes on the part of the leadership.

It becomes clear, therefore, that no cut and dry policy for decision making can always be effectively followed. Decisions differ. As a general rule, however, the following guidelines will assist leaders in making decisions:

24 GUIDELINES FOR MAKING DECISIONS

1. Be sure you understand all of the facts. This will usually require time and research.
2. If possible enlist committees to assist in research and data collecting. Properly evaluate all information gathered.
3. Listen to all possible views (the objectors as well as the positive statements must be considered).
4. Pray diligently about it. God will give you wisdom if you ask for it (James 1:5).
5. Study any biblical teaching that may relate to the matter. We must always go by God's word. (If it has spoken on the matter.)
6. Do not procrastinate. "Indecision is NO decision."
7. Be sure you have considered every alternative. There may be another way, or a better way. Be lateral in your thinking.
8. Be sure you are right and then move ahead.
9. If possible brainstorm the problem for possible solutions.
10. Do not be afraid of your intuition. Many times this is good "information" coming from your subconscious. (Be careful in this area.)
11. Try to be consistent in all areas. Do not leave any loopholes.
12. Do not make a decision solely upon your emotions. They could be wrong or prejudiced.
13. Do not overlook the value of a try-out period. This will give a tentative or possible solution an opportunity to be tested.

14. Be sure all decisions are FULLY communicated to every person involved.
15. Try to get the executioners of the decision to feel like it is their decision. This will take skill and motivation. This becomes easier the more persons you have participating in the decision process.
16. Consider a possible compromise. That is, as long as it involves only matters of opinions. Scripture must not be compromised!
17. After you make the decision stand behind it.
18. Always consider the conditions. It may not be the time for such a decision. (This requires honesty.)
19. Remember, indecision may cause greater problems.
20. Be sure you have the authority to carry out the decision.
21. Do not try to avoid the issue(s). Face facts head on.
22. Hire an expert or seek outside help if necessary. Many decisions should not be made until this is done.
23. Consider all possible consequences. (Do not be afraid of them if you are right.)
24. Never fail to admit that you have been wrong or have made a mistake. This is human. (Do not be stubborn.)

May God bless you with integrity and wisdom as you move ahead in this awesome area of responsibility. All great leaders have done the same thing. It is not an easy task but it is an essential task. Do your best; don't let fear and worry prevent you from being a decisive person. "Decision determines destiny." "History is made when you make a decision." Be a decision man!

LEADERS MUST DELEGATE

Webster defines delegation as, "The act of delegating or condition of being delegated"; and *delegate* as, "One authorized to act as a representative for another or others." These words are very important to the function of leadership. One of the important functions of leadership is the delegating of responsibilities to other persons. This is important because a few leaders cannot do everything that should be done within a congregation. It is also important because it involves many persons in the work of the church; it gives them a chance to use and develop their abilities. For delegation to be successful, it must be approached properly. The following check list is designed to aid you in the work of delegating:

SOME FUNCTIONAL QUALITIES OF LEADERSHIP

Yes No (Check One)
- ☐ ☐ Is this task being assigned just because I (we) don't want to do it?
- ☐ ☐ Has every detail been clearly stated and explained?
- ☐ ☐ Has proper authority been given to insure success?
- ☐ ☐ Has the congregation been informed about this person's responsibility?
- ☐ ☐ Is the person capable of doing the job?
- ☐ ☐ Has the person been successful on other occasions?
- ☐ ☐ Is there a better qualified person for the job?
- ☐ ☐ Has the person been properly trained?
- ☐ ☐ Does the person know of possible dangers?
- ☐ ☐ Does the person know how his job relates to others?
- ☐ ☐ Is the person faithful in all areas of his service to the Lord?
- ☐ ☐ Does the person have questionable habits?
- ☐ ☐ Will the person need money to fulfill his assignment?
- ☐ ☐ Has appropriate money been alloted?
- ☐ ☐ Has an accounting procedure been outlined?
- ☐ ☐ Are special materials needed and are they available?
- ☐ ☐ Is there a deadline?
- ☐ ☐ Does the person know the deadline date?
- ☐ ☐ Does the person know to whom he is responsible?
- ☐ ☐ Does he have a written description of the job?
- ☐ ☐ Will there be periodical reports?
- ☐ ☐ Will the person be left alone until the task is completed?
- ☐ ☐ Is the person in complete control of the "how" the job will be accomplished?
- ☐ ☐ Is the person happy with the assignment?
- ☐ ☐ Does the person know that some parts of his job are confidential?

LEADERS MUST COMMUNICATE

Of all the challenges faced by leadership none is greater than communication. Many problems arise because of failures in this area. Failures come for two major reasons: (1) leaders communicate poorly; (2) leaders do not communicate at all. Even trying at their best, good leaders will face many barriers on the road of communication. Therefore, it is essential that leaders apply themselves diligently to learning and practicing this fine and needful art.

Webster defines *communicate* as, "to impart; pass along; transmit; to make known;" and *communication* as, "a transmitting; a giving, or receiving." Leaders, therefore, are faced with the challenge of sending out words, understood to mean one thing by them, hoping they will be received, interpreted, and understood to mean the same thing by those who receive them. If this takes place, communication is taking place; if it does not, communication is not taking place.

Leaders must seek to communicate for some of the following reasons:

(1) The Bible is a book that requires communication. It must be taught to others.

(2) People must understand the thoughts and ideas of leaders.

(3) Leaders are always trying to gain favorable responses.

(4) Leaders try to get others to agree and act accordingly.

(5) Poor communications produce problems, strife and endangers growth.

(6) Understanding is not an easy thing. It requires work.

(7) Good communications insure favorable attitudes among the followers.

(8) There has been a general lack of communication between followers and leaders

(9) There is a need for interaction between leaders and followers.

(10) Progress and happiness depend upon good communications.

(11) Because of the complaint, "We don't know what is going on."

(12) An atmosphere of secrecy is not good for growth.

Communication, as you well know, is a very delicate process. It is a constant challenge for any leadership. Leaders need to know some of the barriers they may face when trying to communicate, because there are a number which hinder effective communication. Some of these contributors to communication breakdowns are (If a speaker or listener possess any of these they will hinder):

SOME FUNCTIONAL QUALITIES OF LEADERSHIP 43

(1) A harsh tone
(2) Resentments
(3) Prejudices
(4) Hostilities
(5) Defensiveness
(6) Fears
(7) Closedmindedness
(8) Dogmatic attitude
(9) Inconsiderate
(10) Inconsistent
(11) Too emotional
(12) Educational background
(13) Ability to reason
(14) Pride
(15) Set in ways
(16) Followers don't know leaders
(17) Not listening

Try to avoid these pitfalls on the communication road. Be sure, also, to incorporate the following positive qualities because they will aid in communication:

(1) Be a good listener. James wrote, ". . . be swift to hear . . ." (James 1:19).
(2) Think before you speak. James wrote, ". . . be slow to speak . . ." (James 1:19).
(3) Be patient. It takes time to communicate.
(4) Use repetition. A one time statement may not do the Job. Repeat it often.
(5) Be sincere. It will show if you are not.
(6) Trust others. It will encourage them as you communicate.
(7) Practice the attributes of love in I Corinthians 13.
(8) Be kind in your statement of facts.
(9) Be willing to do what you ask others to do.
(10) Be prayerful as you enter into discussions.
(11) Be careful to clarify all points.
(12) Illustrate when necessary. "A picture is worth a thousand words."
(13) Realize the importance of questions (asking and answering).
(14) Be personal. Don't appear or act removed.
(15) Always be Christ-like. (Try to do what Jesus would do.)
(16) Be willing to go the second mile.
(17) Use the printed page. Published messages and decisions may be read and reread.
(18) Plan retreats and special sessions for communication purposes.
(19) Do not take understanding for granted. Not everyone will understand.
(20) Do not present too many subjects or topics at one time.

Pledge yourself to the task of communication. Never take it for granted. It requires constant prayer, effort and thought. Even then, there will be misunderstandings. Always ask yourself these two questions: (1) am I communicating? (2) did I communicate? Good communications will insure good leadership.

FOR DISCUSSION

1. Why is it hard for some persons to make decisions?
2. What is the hardest decision you have ever had to make?
3. Why is decision making important to church leadership?
4. Discuss some good decision makers you have known.
5. Why is indecision dangerous?
6. List some routine decisions you have to make every day.
7. Why are emergency decisions challenging?
8. Discuss some emergency decisions you know about. How were they handled?
9. Do we ever make decisions under pressure? Is this good? Why?
10. Why are innovation decisions sometimes difficult?
11. List other guidelines for making decisions not listed in text.
12. Why do some leaders try to do everything?
13. Why does delegation sometimes fail?
14. Why should leaders delegate?
15. What additional points should be added to the delegation check list?
16. Why should leaders be extra careful in communications?
17. Give an example of a problem produced by poor or no communication.
18. Do members of the congregation have the right to know why various decisions are made? Why? How does communication enter into this area?
19. List additional reasons why leaders need to communicate with great care.
20. Discuss the listed barriers to communications.
21. List any other barriers you may know of relative to communication.
22. Discuss the positive qualities of communications.
23. What are the three most important qualities in communications?
24. Do you consider yourself a good communicator? Why?
25. What do you personally plan to do to improve your communicating ability?

LESSON SEVEN

Leaders Must Plan

INTRODUCTION

For the church to fulfill her mission in the world, leaders must pray and plan for success. Contrary to the thinking of some, planning is a biblical principle. Jesus said, "For which of you intending to build a tower, sitteth down FIRST, and counteth the cost, whether he have sufficient to finish it" (Luke 14:28). This is a very clear picture of planning. Paul taught in Ephesians 1:3-7 that God planned to save men in Christ before the foundation of the world. Luke's account of the great commission sets forth a proper procedure for preaching the gospel to the entire world, i.e., ". . . among all nations, beginning at Jerusalem (Luke 24:47). Isaiah stated that, "The Lord of hosts has sworn: As I have planned, so shall it be, and as I have purposed, so shall it stand" (Isaiah 14:24, RSV). Proper planning, therefore, is approved by God: "Commit your work to the Lord, and your plans will be established" (Proverbs 16:3, RSV).

SIX MAJOR OBJECTIVES OF PLANNING

Someone has rightly said, "Nothing of importance is ever done without a plan." And Henrietta C. Mears was on target when she said, "There is no magic in little plans." Because if God is our partner, we should make large plans. Thus, a good leader will realize the following six major objectives as he launches into big plans for the Lord's work:

(1) Planning must take into consideration WHAT should be done.
(2) Planning must decide WHY it should be done.
(3) Planning determines WHERE it should be done.
(4) Planning decides WHEN it should be done.
(5) Planning determines WHO should do it.
(6) Planning decides HOW it should be done.

Webster defines *plan* as, "an outline; draft; map. A scheme for making, doing, or arranging something. Project or purpose." As leaders of the Lord's church this is what we must do. There is no greater work than His work. As leaders who place our faith and trust in Christ, we believe that we "can do ALL THINGS through Christ who strengthens us" (Phil. 4:12). With God's help, therefore, we can properly handle the objectives of planning.

INGREDIENTS OF PLANNING PROCESS

The following steps are involved in a successful planning process. The leader would do well to note and follow them carefully.

(1) The basic *philosophy* must be considered. This involves determining basic goals and purposes. These will give justification and validity to the overall planning effort. Remember, in many cases the basic philosophy has been established by the Scriptures.

(2) The next major ingredient is determining the specific *objectives* which must be met in order to insure accomplishment of the goals.

(3) The *program* is another important factor in planning. The program will contain the "what" that must be done to achieve the desired results.

(4) *Organization* is an important ingredient in planning. This will determine the human resources which must be enlisted to implement and carry out the program.

(5) Next, you must choose *the staff* or person who will coordinate, organize and lead the way. This will insure the programs function as intended.

(6) A survey of the *facilities* must be made. This is done to determine the number, kind, and location of facilities necessary to carry out the program.

(7) How much will it cost? The *financing* is now to be considered. What are the operating and capital funds necessary to underwrite the entire program? Be sure, therefore, in your planning to consider (a) the philosophy, (b) the objectives, (c) the program, (d) the organization, (e) the staffing, (f) the facilities, and (g) the financing. These are the key ingredients for successful planning.

SOME MECHANICS OF PLANNING

Skillful planning, with God's help, can guarantee success.

Plans succeed because the essentials or ingredients of success are built into the plans. Planning, when properly understood, is the act of cultivating the existing circumstances favorable to the next decision and subsequent decisions. The following practical points should be remembered when entering into a planning session:

WE MUST MAKE AN HONEST SELF-APPRAISAL
(This can be accomplished by asking the following questions:)
(1) Where do we presently stand?
(2) What are our assets and liabilities?
(3) What are our present goals? Spiritually? Physically?
(4) Do we have any definitive aims?
(5) What are our short range goals?
(6) What are our long range goals?
(7) Are our goals tangible or intangible at this time?
(8) Are we motivated?
(9) Are we working diligently?
(10) Is there a spirit of cooperation?
(11) Are we enthusiastic?
(12) Have we been successful in the past?

WE MUST FOCUS OUR THINKING AND PLANNING ON SPECIFICS
(1) We must plan immediate goals as well as long range ones.
(2) We must remember, "Low aim is only self concept expressing itself." Aim high!
(3) We must be specific in our goals. We must write them down.
(4) We must dedicate ourselves with singleness of heart to reach these goals.
(5) Each person involved must have a personal plan of action. Do you have one?

WE MUST DEVELOP A PLAN FOR REACHING OUR GOALS
(1) A detail map must be drawn with the "how" to get there stated very clearly.
(2) We must set a deadline for reaching the goal(s).
(3) We must list ALL possible obstacles to our goal and how to get around them.
(4) We must pinpoint our strength, weakness, assets and liabilities. We must determine where we are and where we want to go.

(5) We must see every problem as a challenge.
(6) With God's help we CAN DO all things. We cannot fail!!

WE MUST HAVE A SINCERE DESIRE FOR THE LORD'S WORK TO SUCCEED

(1) This will give added strength for reaching the goals.
(2) Try to encourage each member of the congregation to examine himself and ask: (a) What are the obstacles I must overcome for the plan to work? (b) What are the plans? Do I know them all? (c) What are the rewards? (d) Is it worth it?

WE MUST MAINTAIN CONFIDENCE IN GOD AND BRETHREN

(1) Confidence submits itself to obstacles and overcomes them.
(2) Confidence stimulates creative imagination. We will never do it until we think we can.
(3) Confidence, therefore, in God and brethren will guarantee success.
(4) "We either succeed at failure, or succeed at success."
(5) "Will we think big or will we think small?" Confidence will determine!

WE MUST DEVELOP DETERMINATION TO FOLLOW THROUGH WITH PLANS

(1) No matter what others do, I will follow through.
(2) No matter what they think, I will follow through.
(3) No matter what obstacles arise, I will follow through.
(4) I know that it is easy to make plans, but hard to follow through.
(5) It is easy to get excited in a crowd, or at a pep talk. But to succeed in the long run, there must be constant personal motivation. Do you have it?

WE MUST REMEMBER THE PITFALLS

(1) Considering financing to be the first step.
(2) Determining the personnel or facilities BEFORE the program is written.
(3) Failure to creatively involve the kinds of people necessary to do the jobs.
(4) Failure to secure proper help and staffing.

BRAINSTORMING AND PLANNING

A very important tool in planning is brainstorming. Webster defines brainstorming as, "the unrestrained offering of ideas by all members of a group meeting as in a business planning conference." From such a session comes many valuable benefits.

VALUE OF BRAINSTORMING

(1) Involves each person in the group (The shy person will find himself involved before he knows it).
(2) Promotes enthusiasm and excitement (The many possibilities will be encouraging).
(3) Stimulates the minds of all present (Will help to draw from subconscious).
(4) Produces many new ideas that are good and worthwhile (It will also revive old ideas).
(5) Promotes creativity and use of imagination.
(6) Important key in achieving success.
(7) Several heads are better than one.

SOME GUIDELINES FOR BRAINSTORMING

(1) Be sure each participant understands the purpose of a brainstorming session.
(2) Do not criticize anyone's comment (This is not the purpose of brainstorming. Let each person speak freely).
(3) Be spontaneous (Say what you think).
(4) Seek as much quantity as possible (50 ideas are better than 15).
(5) Build upon the ideas of others (Their comments will provoke deeper thoughts and better ideas).
(6) Record all ideas that are presented (May be done in writing, tape recorder).
(7) Set a time limit (The pressure of time produces results. An open-ended session will drag on and on).
(8) Have a leader (chairman) to direct the session.
(9) At a later date evaluate the ideas one by one (Select a committee. Don't neglect a single idea).
(10) Never conclude that a problem or need is too small for brainstorming. It will amaze you at the things that may be brought out relative to a so-called unimportant problem (We are not advocating that brainstorming be reduced to an exercise in trivials).
(11) State each problem as clearly as possible. Be sure it is fully understood.

(12) Present and storm one idea or problem at a time (Do not get sidetracked).
(13) Present any known data you may have relative to the subject.
(14) All participants must readily identify with the issue under storming.
(15) Statements relative to the issue must not be taken personally by another participant.
(16) The leader should launch the session, if possible, by presenting one or two ideas. (Or he may simply state the problem).
(17) Pray for wisdom (James 1:2-5).

Add brainstorming to your planning sessions. It will produce results that you will be pleased with. It is a must for good planning.

CONCLUSION

There is a great work to be done by the Lord's people. The ever vital question is HOW to accomplish this work. Much study, prayer, sacrifice and planning must go into it; especially, by the leadership. Goals must be set with an organized plan for reaching them. This will require many long hours of hard work. But it is worth it because it involves the greatest work in the world.

In closing the following words by Daniel H. Burnham, former Chicago architect and city planner, reminds us of the challenge before us:

> "Make no little plans: they have no magic to stir men's blood and probably themselves will not be realized. Make big plans; aim high in hope and work, remembering that a noble, logical diagram once recorded will never die, but long after we are gone will be a living thing, asserting itself with ever-growing insistency. Remember our sons and grandsons are going to do things that would stagger us. Let your watchword be order and your beacon beauty. Think big. Remember that when you create a situation that captures the imagination, you capture life, everything."

Words like WORLD, EVERY CREATURE, HEAVEN, ETERNAL LIFE, HELL, etc., remind us that our Lord has taught us to THINK BIG. Therefore, we must PLAN and act accordingly.

LEADERS MUST PLAN

FOR DISCUSSION

1. Why is planning essential to church growth?
2. Why is planning neglected?
3. Is it scriptural to plan? Why?
4. Discuss I Corinthians 14:40 in relation to planning.
5. What is an objective?
6. What is meant by philosophy of planning?
7. How does a program relate to planning?
8. Why is organization important to planning?
9. When is the last time your church had a planning session?
10. When should financing be considered in planning?
11. Why is self-appraisal necessary?
12. List from memory the major mechanics of planning.
13. When should a congregation start planning? How often should they have planning sessions?
14. Should plans ever be changed? Why?
15. Why should plans be put into writing?
16. Have you ever been in a brainstorming session?
17. Create, in class, some possible situation, e.g., need for new building, problem with busing program, lack of parking, advertisement for meeting, etc., and brainstorm it.
18. Use brainstorming in your next planning session.
19. Do you know of any weaknesses in brainstorming? What?
20. Does your church have 1 - 5 - 10 - 15 - 20 year plans?
21. What is the biggest hindrance to planning?
22. Why should we make BIG plans?
23. Why should a number of persons be involved in planning sessions?
24. Do you fully understand the benefits of brainstorming?
25. Discuss Luke 14:24 and its relationship to planning.

LESSON EIGHT
Leaders Must Set Goals

INTRODUCTION

Not only must leaders be involved in planning the Lord's work, they must also be involved in planning their day to day personal lives. This gets down to goal setting on a personal basis. What are the goals of your life? I do not mean in just *one* area but all areas. What are your spiritual goals? What are your vocational goals? What are your leadership goals? What are your social goals? What are your family goals? What are your financial goals? These, and other areas of life, are important to personal health, success and happiness. A leader will be successful in direct proportion to his personal planning and goal setting habits. Purpose, therefore, is a vital key to achievement. When you set a personal goal you have established a concrete objective, which is measurable over a definite period of time.

PERSONAL GOALS

How about you, do you have a written list of life goals? Have you taken time to write down the things, with God's help, you hope to accomplish in your alloted three score and ten years? If yes, have you been careful to keep these goals current, relative to their priority? If you do not have such a list, you need to make one, now!

There are many ways to approach goal setting. The following model will serve to illustrate goal setting in the area of family relations:

LEADERS MUST SET GOALS

PURPOSE: To be a better husband.
OBJECTIVE: To be more considerate of my wife.
Goal: 1. To pick up my clothes and other items I normally leave behind.
Fulfillment approach:
   a. I was careful to put my dirty clothing into the hamper.
   b. I put the newspaper in the garbage when I was finished.
   c. I encouraged the children to do likewise.
   d. I even picked up some of my wife's clothes.

Goal: 2. To show my wife more love.
Fulfillment approach:
   a. I sent her some roses.
   b. I told her, "I love you." (over the phone, etc.)
   c. I practiced being courteous.

Goal: 3. To purchase some work saving item.
Fulfillment approach:
   a. I saved five dollars per payday.
   b. I cut a picture out of the paper of the item and placed it in my wallet.
   c. I bought her a dishwasher.

No matter what approach you take in goal setting it will contain the above ingredients, even though they may be stated differently, etc. You can take the above example, therefore, and adapt it to every area of your personal life. It will work if you will work!

Personal goal setting and planning is just as challenging as goal setting and planning on the congregational level. Thus, we need some workable guidelines in this area, too. In setting personal goals remember the following points:

First, work on setting one goal at a time. Be specific; and be sure it is the most meaningful goal for you at this time in your life. Crystallize your thinking and move ahead with singleness of purpose. Keep your eyes on the target.

Second, write your goal down. State it in clear, honest, understandable terms. Do not fool yourself or be too spiritual. Seeing your goal on paper will give you visual motivation.

Third, think about your goal frequently (daily). Take the paper you have written your goal on and look at it several times a day. Form a mental picture of your goal and your achieving it.

Fourth, set a deadline for reaching your goal. Do not use the nebulous "someday" approach. "Someday" will never come. Set the month and year you plan for your goal to be reached. Some men go so far as to set the day and month.

Fifth, do not be discouraged. It is very human to become discouraged. The key is do not let it be turned into defeat. Keep a burning desire to achieve your goal. Be confident, God will help. Nothing can defeat determination!

Sixth, be willing to make changes. No one knows what shall be on the tomorrow (James 4:14-18). Therefore, many unexpected things may come up as you move toward your goal. You must be flexible and change when necessary. Be sure, however, that changes do not alter your goal (if the goal is still possible).

Seventh, work diligently each day. This is a major key in reaching your goal. Approach it with enthusiasm. Remember, it is worth your work and energy.

Eighth, remember it is exciting and youthful to always have something ahead to look forward to. A person without a plan and goal in life is not long for life. Emerson rightly said, "We do not count a man's years, until he has nothing else to count." A person with a goal will always have something to count.

Ninth, be sure you have all of the essential facts. This is why goal setting and planning involves time. You will need all the facts before you launch out on the road toward your goal. Do your homework. Get the facts.

Tenth, remember the various levels of planning and goal setting. Goals are of great variety and levels. Some of these levels are: (a) your total life goals; (b) your 5 - 10 - 15 year plan; (c) your plans for a year; (d) your plans for six months; (e) your plans for a month; (f) your plans for a week; (g) your plans for a day; (h) your plans for several hours. This is known as long and short range planning. You must do both.

Eleventh, be sure to properly approach your DAILY plans. The following suggestions will help you to prepare a goal list for each day: (a) write tomorrow's goals tonight. These are the "things to do" items; (b) pray over them, asking God to help; (c) list each goal according to importance; (d) look at your list in the morning before you depart for work; (e) start to work on your number one item; (f) review your goals at lunch (you may also look at your long range goal list); (g) make any adjustments if needed; (h) review when work day is over; (i) evaluate the list before going to bed; (j) prepare tomorrow's list, etc.

Twelfth, pray for wisdom; study the Scriptures and move ahead with God as your helper.

PERSONAL IMPROVEMENT

"Everyone can do something to make the world better. He can at least improve himself."

"People seldom improve when they have no other model but themselves to copy after" (Oliver Goldsmith).

"The biggest room in the world is the room for improvement."

"If you are still breathing, you can improve."

The above thoughts stress the importance of self improvement. For the leader who seeks to be the very best, this is a must. Daily goal setting will assist in this area. Use or adapt the following plan for a one month period. It will aid you in personal development. (These are merely suggestions. Make your own.)

ONE MONTH PERSONAL IMPROVEMENT PLAN

Between now and_____, I will

A. *With God's help break these habits:*
1. Stop procrastinating.
2. Break the smoking habit (if you have it.)
3. Free my vocabulary of negative remarks, etc.
4. Make better use of my time. I will not watch too much TV.
5. Refrain from talking about people.
6. Not be late for an appointment or church service.
7. Drop my "wait and see attitude."

B. *With God's help, seek to acquire these habits:*
(If you don't have them, etc.)
1. Smile and be friendly to everyone I come in contact with.
2. Sincerely compliment people at every opportunity.
3. Do something good for a person I am having difficulty with.
4. Check my daily goal list each morning.
5. Carry out my daily plan and goals.
6. Make the best use of my time by keeping a schedule.
7. Develop the spirit of "praying without ceasing." (I Thess. 5:17).

C. *Increase my value to the congregation in these ways:*
   1. Do a better job in all areas of responsibility.
   2. Learn more of God's word.
   3. Be a better example for others to follow.
   4. Make four positive suggestions for congregational improvement.
   5. Being dependable in every situation.
   6. Be a better prepared teacher, preacher, etc.
   7. Be ready unto every good work.
D. *Be a better person in the home in these ways:*
   1. Show more appreciation for my wife; especially, in relation to the many little things she does. I will not take her for granted.
   2. At least once a week, I will do something special with the family.
   3. Give one hour each day (or more) to the children.
   4. Help develop a more spiritual atmosphere around the house.
   5. Do repair work that has been neglected.
   6. Clean out the garage.
   7. Practice respect for each member of my family.
E. *Develop my mind in these ways:*
   1. Study a minimum of two hours each week in the field of leadership.
   2. Study the Bible daily.
   3. Attend a lectureship or seminar.
   4. Read a good self-help book.
   5. Try to make four new friends.
   6. Tell five persons that I appreciate them.
   7. Spend thirty minutes daily in quiet, reflective thinking.
   8. Dream "impossible" dreams.
   9. Imagine the church reaching four specific goals.
F. *Develop more Christ-likeness in these ways:*
   1. Forgive someone that has wronged me.
   2. Love someone who does not love me (as far as you can tell)
   3. Pray for three missionaries by name.
   4. Visit three persons who are shut-in.
   5. Practice the golden rule.
   6. Encourage three weak Christians.
   7. Teach someone the gospel.

LEADERS MUST SET GOALS

These suggested areas of personal improvement, may or may not fit your mood or needs. Take them as a model, then, and develop your own one month program. Do not drop it after a month; keep it up from now on. You will be the winner. Each member should share his progress with the class (if this is studied in class).

FOR DISCUSSION

1. How do personal plans and goals relate to church planning?
2. Do you have a list of personal goals?
3. Have you always set goals and worked toward them?
4. Below list four major life goals (following the text model):

PURPOSE:

OBJECTIVE:

GOAL: 1.

Fulfillment
approach: a.
                 b.
                 c.

GOAL: 2.
Fulfillment
approach: a.
                 b.
                 c.

GOAL: 3.
Fulfillment
approach: a.
                 b.
                 c.

GOAL: 4.
Fulfillment
approach: a.
                 b.
                 c.

5. Using the above model prepare a set of goals for a year in the area of leadership.
6. Using the above model prepare a set of goals for a week in the area of personal evangelism (or any other area).
7. Prepare a list of goals for tomorrow. Be specific. Report your progress.
8. Prepare a list of goals you would like to see your congregation reach. Share these with the class (or others).
9. Do you have a notebook to write your goals down in?
10. How do goals keep a person "young"?
11. List the various levels of goal setting.
12. Why should you set a deadline?
13. How does writing a goal down help a person reach it?
14. Have you prepared your month improvement program?
15. Why do we need wisdom in goal setting?
16. Do you have goals for your job (secular)?
17. Do you have financial goals?
18. Do you have personal improvement goals for your job?
19. Are you excited about goal setting? Why?
20. Will you stick to the task of goal setting? Why would you quit?

LESSON NINE

Leaders Must Evaluate

INTRODUCTION

Businesses, government agencies, educational institutions, and denominational churches spend a lot of time, energy and money on self-studies. These studies pinpoint strong areas as well as problem and weak areas. After a thorough analysis the institution plots and launches a course designed to eliminate the weaknesses as well as insure continual growth. But for some reason this sound business approach has not been used within the Lord's church (there may be a few exceptions). Why haven't we analyzed ourselves? Perhaps leadership is to blame or we may be afraid to find out the real condition of the congregation. If a congregation is to grow, it must do a self-study. For a self-evaluation to be beneficial it must be more than just a collection of facts, statistics and categories. These things merely provide the facts. Action must be taken after the facts have been presented. Therefore, the information will be of value only as it is used to plot a future course.

Every church should be concerned with its rate of growth. It must constantly ask these three questions: (1) are we dying? (2) are we maintaining status quo? (3) are we growing? Leadership will never be content until the church has an affirmative answer to the third question — YES! WE ARE GROWING.

IS OUR CONGREGATION DYING, MAINTAINING STATUS QUO, OR GROWING?

1. The following areas of inquiry will help answer this question. (To fully benefit from this self-study will require diligent work in gathering all the facts and figures).

60 LEADERSHIP AND CHURCH GROWTH

A. A congregation is dying, status quo, or growing in direct proportion to its attendance and membership increase or decrease from year to year. In the following spaces give the requested information from the past five years:

Attendance At Worship Services

Sunday morning	Sunday night	Wednesday night
1. _____	1. _____	1. _____
2. _____	2. _____	2. _____
3. _____	3. _____	3. _____
4. _____	4. _____	4. _____
5. _____	5. _____	5. _____

Attendance In Bible Classes

Sunday morning	Vacation Bible School	Others
1. _____	1. _____	1. _____
2. _____	2. _____	2. _____
3. _____	3. _____	3. _____
4. _____	4. _____	4. _____
5. _____	5. _____	5. _____

Membership during last five years: (Add monthly to get yearly)
1. _____
2. _____
3. _____
4. _____
5. _____

How many baptisms during each of the past five years
1. _____
2. _____
3. _____
4. _____
5. _____

* Give percentage of these baptisms who had no prior contact with church.

LEADERS MUST EVALUATE

B. A congregation is dying, status quo, or growing in direct proportion to its increase or decrease in contributions (Remember the rate of inflation, salary increases, etc.)

List yearly contribution for past 5 years:

1. _____
2. _____
3. _____
4. _____
5. _____

Give the salary and benefit increases of all church employees (including preacher, janitor, secretary, etc.) for past 5 years:

Position _____
  Salary:
    1. _____   Benefits:
    2. _____
    3. _____
    4. _____
    5. _____

How much did the congregation give to foreign mission work in past 5 years?

1. _____
2. _____
3. _____
4. _____
5. _____

How much did the congregation give to local mission work in past 5 years?

1. _____
2. _____
3. _____
4. _____
5. _____

C. A congregation is dying, status quo, or growing to the extent its benevolence increased or decreased during the past five years.

How much did the congregation give to benevolent work in past five years?

1. _____
2. _____
3. _____
4. _____
5. _____

D. A congregation is dying, status quo, or growing to the degree it is training and providing NEW leaders. Below give the number of new persons added to the various positions of leadership in the past 5 years:

Elders	Deacons	Teachers	Preachers	Song Leaders	Missionaries
1. __	1. __	1. __	1. __	1. __	1. __
2. __	2. __	2. __	2. __	2. __	2. __
3. __	3. __	3. __	3. __	3. __	3. __
4. __	4. __	4. __	4. __	4. __	4. __
5. __	5. __	5. __	5. __	5. __	5. __

Serve Publicly
(Wait on table, make announcements, lead in prayer, etc.)

1. _____
2. _____
3. _____
4. _____
5. _____

E. A congregation is dying, status quo, or growing to the extent its facilities are adequate.

Give the percentage of capacity filled during the past 5 years:

Auditorium	Classrooms
1. __	1. __
2. __	2. __
3. __	3. __
4. __	4. __
5. __	5. __

LEADERS MUST EVALUATE

F. A congregation is dying, status quo, or growing to the extent it is KEEPING its new converts.

Below give the number of converts for each of the past five years and the number still faithful:

Converted	Still Faithful
1. ___	1. ___
2. ___	2. ___
3. ___	3. ___
4. ___	4. ___
5. ___	5. ___

G. A church is dying, status quo, or growing to the extent the members are growing in Bible knowledge (this also includes children). Prepare a basic Bible test for each group within the congregation. Be brief and simple.

H. A congregation is dying, status quo, or growing to the extent its members are teaching and baptizing the lost.

List the baptisms for each of the five past years and the number of persons responsible for them:

Baptisms	Persons Involved In Teaching
1. ___	1. ___
2. ___	2. ___
3. ___	3. ___
4. ___	4. ___
5. ___	5. ___

* How many members, based on the above facts, did it take to baptize one person? Divide the number of converts into the number of members to get this percentage.

AN EVALUATION CHECKLIST

The following information will contribute to the above evaluation. It will help pinpoint many other areas essential to church growth. With much thought and deliberation, as well as with correct information, check the answer appropriate for the question.

Yes No (Check One)

☐ ☐ 1. Is every program evangelistic?
☐ ☐ 2. Do all members attend all services of the church?
☐ ☐ 3. Does the contribution represent at least 10% of the membership's income?
☐ ☐ 4. Does the congregation have a good educational program in stewardship?
☐ ☐ 5. Are members constantly reminded of the various programs of the church?
☐ ☐ 6. Do Bible classes have more members than the congregation membership?
☐ ☐ 7. Do you have a planned program to recruit new Bible school students?
☐ ☐ 8. Are all teachers faithful in attending services?
☐ ☐ 9. Do all teachers have good life habits? (no smoking, etc.)
☐ ☐ 10. Do teachers visit pupils regularly?
☐ ☐ 11. Does the congregation always have home Bible studies in progress?
☐ ☐ 12. Has every home in your neighborhood been visited?
☐ ☐ 13. Do you keep and display adequate tracts in neighborhood businesses?
☐ ☐ 14. Does the congregation keep complete records of members?
☐ ☐ 15. Does the congregation have an efficient system for registering visitors?
☐ ☐ 16. Do you have a program to visit all visitors?
☐ ☐ 17. Do you conduct a yearly religious census?
☐ ☐ 18. Do you have a system for checking weekly on newcomers to town?
☐ ☐ 19. Does the congregation conduct a yearly Vacation Bible School?
☐ ☐ 20. Does the congregation have at least two gospel meetings each year?
☐ ☐ 21. Do you have at least two other special learning or study programs each year?
☐ ☐ 22. Do ushers help persons find seats, etc.?
☐ ☐ 23. Are all visitors greeted?
☐ ☐ 24. Does the congregation have a weekly visitation program?

LEADERS MUST EVALUATE

Yes No (Check One)

- ☐ ☐ 25. Are teachers helped to grow by a special program each year?
- ☐ ☐ 26. Does the congregation support one missionary for each 100 members?
- ☐ ☐ 27. Does the congregation carry on a good advertising program year round?
- ☐ ☐ 28. Is there a comprehensive benevolent program?
- ☐ ☐ 29. Do elders, deacons, preachers receive some type of training or help each year to guarantee constant growth?
- ☐ ☐ 30. Are the young men and boys given proper training?
- ☐ ☐ 31. Do you have up-to-date Bible school records?
- ☐ ☐ 32. Do you have an active prospect file?
- ☐ ☐ 33. Does the congregation have well equipped classrooms?
- ☐ ☐ 34. Does the congregation have ample parking?
- ☐ ☐ 35. Does every member have an assigned job or responsibility?
- ☐ ☐ 36. Do you have 1 - 5 - 10 - 15 - 20 years plans? (Circle one.)
- ☐ ☐ 37. Is the minister and other employees given salary increases each year?
- ☐ ☐ 38. Is there an up-to-date membership directory?
- ☐ ☐ 39. Is office space sufficient?
- ☐ ☐ 40. Is there a church library?
- ☐ ☐ 41. Is there a weekly bulletin?
- ☐ ☐ 42. Is a secretary needed in the church office?
- ☐ ☐ 43. Are regular fellowship opportunities provided?
- ☐ ☐ 44. Does the congregation conduct a correspondence course?
- ☐ ☐ 45. Do members receive a good Christian magazine (e.g., 20th Century Christian; Christian Family Magazine, etc.)
- ☐ ☐ 46. Does the congregation have enough charts and film strips available for cottage meetings?
- ☐ ☐ 47. Is a personal work class conducted yearly?
- ☐ ☐ 48. Is there a new converts' class?
- ☐ ☐ 49. Is there a local radio or TV program sponsored by the congregation?

Yes No (Check One)
- ☐ ☐ 50. Do senior citizens have special activities?
- ☐ ☐ 51. Does the ladies' Bible class meet year round?
- ☐ ☐ 52. Is there a hospital visitation program?
- ☐ ☐ 53. Is there a nursing home visitation program?
- ☐ ☐ 54. Are teenagers used in various programs?
- ☐ ☐ 55. Do you have a bus program?
- ☐ ☐ 56. Is there a special class on marriage and the home conducted at least once a year?
- ☐ ☐ 57. Does the congregation practice discipline of ungodly members?
- ☐ ☐ 58. Does the congregation have a teachers' work room?
- ☐ ☐ 59. Are men appointed to serve in the worship services a month in advance?
- ☐ ☐ 60. Is your budget being met each Sunday?

CONCLUSION

You should now be in a better position to plan the future of your congregation. Do not be discouraged if the evaluation showed a number of problems. You need to know the truth. This will aid you in planning the future. Likewise, you should not be too content if the evaluation looks favorable. Determine in either case to MOVE FORWARD during the coming twelve months. With God's help, great things will happen in your congregation. Today is the day to begin. Start now!

FOR DISCUSSION

1. Why is evaluation important to church growth?
2. When was the last date you conducted an evaluation of your congregation?_____
3. Have you completed the five year evaluation self-study?
4. Why do some congregations refuse to evaluate themselves?
5. Why should leaders be concerned with church growth?
6. What do you plan to do with the results of the congregation checklist?
7. Can you think of other items that should be added to the 60 points?
8. Why is it helpful to pinpoint our problems?
9. Are you ready to launch into a dynamic planning program for the future of the congregation?
10. Where will you go from here?

LESSON TEN

Leaders And Church Growth (I)

INTRODUCTION

In our last study we zeroed in on planning for church growth via evaluation. In this lesson, and the one that follows, we want to give some additional time to several points that were touched on in the evaluation lesson. Leaders must be interested in growing dynamic, active churches for the Lord.

It is a biblical truth that the Lord has the responsibility of adding the saved to the church (Cf. Acts 2:47; I Corinthians 12:18). The Lord does this work in direct proportion to our teaching and converting the lost. If the church fails in her mission of preaching the gospel, God is not able to add the saved to His family. Likewise, the church (saved people) grows spiritually to the degree of edification received by each member of the body. Just as God intends for the lost to be evangelized, He, also intends for the saved to be edified (Cf. Ephesians 4:11-16). These are the two areas the church is commanded to grow in: saving the lost, and growing spiritually after one is saved.

Churches do not grow and become strong by chance or haphazard methods. Behind every growing church is a dedicated leadership. Leaders, therefore, must know this and function accordingly. The following principles are vital to church growth. After studying each point make application to your congregational situation.

SOME FACTORS OF CHURCH GROWTH

First, every congregation of God's people must have qualified and dedicated elders. This was pointed out by Paul when he wrote to Titus these words, "For this cause left I thee in Crete, that thou shouldest set in order the things that are wanting (undone, jjt), and ordain elders in every city, as I had appointed" until they meet the qualifications set down by God in I Timothy 3:1-11; Titus 1:5-10. These men must be characterized by faith, dependence on God, vision, wisdom, courage and devotion to God and His cause. They must, also, recognize the nature of their WORK as overseers of the flock (Acts 20:28). It is in this area that many problems occur: many elders do not know what their REAL work is (or many don't do it). In many places the elders do deacons' work and the preacher does the work of the elders. This is why much prayer and study must go into the appointing of elders. Until a congregation has elders, each member must do his best to carry on the Lord's work and qualify men to become elders (actually a man qualifies himself). God ordained that elders lead His church. Nothing short of this arrangement will do. A congregation should conduct an in-depth study in the work and qualification of elders.

Second, the word must be faithfully preached in its wholeness. It must be preached without fear, partiality or malice by a courageous spokesman. Paul wrote, "preach the word; be instant in season, out of season; reprove, rebuke, exhort with all long-suffering and doctrine" (II Timothy 4:2). Like Paul, the preachers of today must declare the WHOLE counsel of God (Acts 20:27). This demands a balanced diet of the word, covering all subjects from A (adultry) to Z (zeal), and all verses from Genesis 1:1 to Revelation 22:21. To do this kind of preaching the local preacher must have time to study and meditate in God's word. Thus, it must be recognized that he cannot do "101" odd jobs and still be prepared to preach the whole counsel of God. Likewise, the preacher must be supported in preaching the whole counsel of God. Paul warned, "For the time will come when they will not endure sound doctrine; but after their own lusts shall they heap to themselves teachers having itching ears" (II Timothy 4:3). Sad to say, in some congregations this is happening. But if you will note carefully, these congregations are not growing. The church will grow if it receives sound preaching. Therefore, leadership must demand it, and followers must rejoice in it. A man dare not call himself a preacher if he preaches less (or more) than the "whole counsel of God." Someone has rightly stated, "As the pulpit goes, so goes the church." The preacher, therefore would do well to remember the following words of Goulburn, "Send

LEADERS AND CHURCH GROWTH (I)

your audience away with a desire for, and an impulse toward spiritual improvement, or your preaching will be a failure." Preaching the whole counsel will insure growth and improvement in every area.

Third, discipline must be practiced. A pure church will be a growing church. A church with "sin in the camp" is failing to be what God intends for her to be. This is another unpopular subject among many brethren. In fact, it is rarely practiced with any consistency by most congregations. The attitude has arisen of peace at any price. "Don't rock the boat," is the favorite expression of many in our day. This is not, however, what God's word says about the subject. It makes it very clear that the disorderly and ungodly must be disciplined. Notice some of the sins that subjects one to discipline if he does not repent:

(1) *Causing divisions:* "Now I beseech you, brethren, mark them which cause divisions and offences contrary to the doctrine which ye have learned; and avoid them" (Romans 16:17).

(2) *Those guilty of fornication:* "But now I have written unto you not to keep company, if any man that is called a brother be a fornicator . . ." (I Cor. 15:11).

(3) *A covetous brother:* ". . . or covetous . . ." (I Cor. 15:11).

(4) *An idolator:* ". . . or an idolator . . ." (I Cor. 5:11).

(5) *Trouble maker:* ". . . or a railer . . ." (I Cor. 5:11).

(6) *A drunkard:* ". . . or a drunkard . . ." (I Cor. 5:11).

(7) *An extortioner:* ". . . or an extortioner . . ." (I Cor. 5:11).

(8) *Those that walk disorderly:* "Now we command you, brethren, in the name of our Lord Jesus Christ, that ye withdraw yourselves from every brother that walketh disorderly, and not after the traditions which he received of us" (II Thess. 3:6).

(9) *Those who defy the truth:* "And if any man obey not our word by this epistle, note that man, and have no company with him, that he may be ashamed" (II Thess. 3:14).

Withdrawing of fellowship should be the last step in trying to get a Christian to return to the Lord. Much prayer, work and time must go before this final act. The directions in Matthew 18:15-20; Galatians 6:1, 2; and James 5:19, 20 should be followed in love and patience. A disciplined church is a growing church. (Discipline, also, warrants a special in-depth study).

Fourth, the importance of each member must be constantly remembered. A church on the move for the Lord recognizes the value of each member. Thus, there are no big "I's" or little "You's" in the Lord's service. Whether one will admit it or not, there are some in the Lord's church who view themselves and others as VIP's in the kingdom. On one occasion I was visiting a couple who had quit coming to church services. As I talked with them, trying to find out why they had stopped, one of them replied: "Oh, you don't need us down there, we're not important . . . you can get along without us." How sad for a member of the body of Christ to feel this way. Some have not been taught how important they are in the body of Christ and the promoting of His work on earth. Good leadership will be careful to avoid this problem by constantly stressing the importance of each member. The Bible makes it very clear that there are no second-class citizens in the church of the Lord. In a sense every member of the church is a VIP. James said that God has chosen the poor to be rich in faith and heirs of the kingdom (James 3:1-8). Paul also pointed out the importance of each member at Corinth when dealing with their problem over spiritual gifts. A look at his words in chapter twelve of First Corinthians will show WHY each member of the body is important:

(1) Each member of the church is important because his placement into the body was an act of God, not man. Paul said, "But now hath God set the members everyone of them in the body, as it hath pleased him" (I Corinthians 12:18). "The Lord added daily to the church such as should be saved" (Acts 2:47). Therefore, how can I treat a brother as none important? I cannot!

(2) Each member of the church is important because variety is needed within the body. Paul said, "For as the body is one, and hath many members, and all the members of that one body, being many, are one body: so also is Christ" (I Corinthians 12:12). The variety is illustrated by Paul in using the human body for a comparison (I Corinthians 12:13-18). The body would be deformed if every member were identical (I Corinthians 12:19-21).

LEADERS AND CHURCH GROWTH (I)

Good leadership will tap the unique ability of each member and put it to work for the Master. Every person has some ability; leaders must be aware of this and act accordingly.

(3) Each member is important even if he is feeble. Paul declared, "Nay much more those members of the body, which seem to be more feeble, are necessary: And those members of the body, which seem to think to be less honorable, upon these bestow more abundant honor; and our uncomely parts have more abundant comeliness" (I Corinthians 12:22, 23). Sometimes in our personal work, we make a special effort to convert Mr. X because of who he is and what he has. In some places the poor and uneducated are made to feel like second-class citizens in the kingdom. This is wrong!

(4) Each member is important because he is cared for by the rest of the members. "And whether one member suffer, all the members suffer with it; or one member is honored, all the members rejoice with it" (I Corinthians 12:26). Just as in the human anatomy one member contributed to another when an injury takes place, so it is within the spiritual body. We care one for another.

(5) Each member is important, as we have stressed before, because he has at least ONE talent (ability) given to him by the Lord (I Corinthians 12:27-31). Every Christian can do something. Just because he does not do what I do, or as much as I do, doesn't mean that he is not acceptable to God. God holds him accountable for what he has, not what he doesn't have. It is the job of leadership to help each member know of his place within the church. A church that does this is a growing church.

Fifth, Christ must be the central factor in all efforts. He must be the drawing power in all programs and plans. Advertisement is a multimillion dollar business. Many hours, weeks, and even years go into developing an appeal to draw consumers to a product. Someone has said, "You can sell anything if you make it attractive enough." Thus everything from soup to soap, beer to aspirin is advertised with the goal of drawing people to them. While leaders of the church are interested in drawing people to Christ and His church, they must not, however, fall into the trap of using nominal or unscriptural drawing powers. Such foundations will not stand.

Religions, down through the years, have also concerned themselves with drawing power. The Judaizers drew followers by coupling the law of Moses with Christ. Gnostics drew followers by permitting lust and salvation. Constantine drew people to the baptismal waters by offering gifts. Charles Taze Russell, founder of the Jehovah's Witnesses, drew people with his doctrines of no hell; no Trinity; no resurrection and judgment. Mary Baker Eddy, founder of Christian Science, drew people by convincing them that pain and sin were not real; satan, death and hell were only states of the mortal mind. Joseph Smith, founder of Mormonism, drew people by convincing them that he was a prophet with a revelation from God. Herbert W. Armstrong, Radio Church of God, draws people with a false hope of a thousand years reign on earth, etc.

Today everything under the sun is being tried in an effort to draw people into churches. Among denominationalist the gamut runs from jazz masses to rock plays. They have tried everything from sports to bingo. They have tried the "social gospel" and the picket line; do-nothing to emotionalism and works. Yet their number continues to dwindle year after year. It is true that such actions draw people for a little while, but, they do not last very long. Why? Obviously something is wrong with the drawing power. Leaders must learn from these lessons.

Among churches of Christ, sad to say, we have tried our hand at using nominal drawing powers, too. Some have thought that a well educated preacher would draw people. Others have cried, "If we only had a new church building we could get people to come." And still others cry, "If we only had a program we could draw people." We have had all of these things for years, and the masses still pass by on the other side. What is wrong? Maybe something is wrong with our drawing power!

As far as Christianity is concerned, Jesus Christ is the sufficient drawing power. Jesus said, "And I, if I be lifted up, shall draw all men unto me" (John 12:32). Initially, the Master meant His being lifted upon a cross would be powerful enough to draw men unto Him (John 12:33). From the day of Pentecost onward, we see the drawing power of Christ demonstrated in the book of Acts. What do you suppose would have happened if Peter had addressed the Jews with an invitation to come later on that night and listen to him preach and then remain for a "fellowship" or game afterwards? I don't believe 3,000 would have returned, much less have obeyed the gospel. Peter challenged them right on the spot, face-to-face, by lifting Christ up as their only hope (Cf. Acts 2:21-47). We must do likewise.

There are several ways we must lift Christ up as our drawing power today. First, he must be lifted up as the content of faithful gospel preaching, because the Good News unto salvation is about Him (Mark 16:15, 16; Romans 1:16; I Corinthians 15:1-4). Second, He must be lifted up as the Christ who demands self-denial of every follower (Matthew 16:24). We dare not require less than the Master does! Third, Jesus must be lifted up as the lover of all men (John 3:16; Revelation 1:5), not just a privileged few. Fourth, He must be lifted up as the Christ who demands obedience (John 14:15; Hebrews 5:8, 9). Fifth, He must be lifted up as the Christ who promises suffering (Matthew 5:12, 13; Philippians 3:10). Nowhere does Jesus promise his followers a "bed of roses". Sixth, He must be lifted up as the helping Christ (Matthew 11:28-32; 28:18-20). He hasn't left His people to sink or swim by their own power. A study of the Bible will reveal additional ways of "lifting Jesus up."

If we are going to draw people to Christ and His church, we must place HIM FIRST in our lives and teaching. Leadership, therefore, must let nothing serve as a substitute drawing power. We are NOT against programs, in fact just the opposite is true. But we must keep Christ as the motivation for every action and plan. Our desire and practice should ever be to lift the Blessed Savior up. HE IS SUFFICIENT!

CONCLUSION

In this lesson we have stressed five important factors in church growth. If the church grows it must have (1) strong elders; (2) faithful preaching of the word; (3) discipline of the ungodly; (4) a recognition of the importance of each member; and (5) Christ as the proper drawing power. Good leadership will be constantly working for proficiency in these areas. In the next lesson we will study some additional factors in church growth.

FOR DISCUSSION

1. What two major areas must the church grow in?
2. Why does God desire for the church to grow?
3. Discuss Ephesians 4:11-16.
4. Why should a congregation have elders?
5. Discuss Hebrews 13:17 relationship to elders.
6. Discuss I Peter 5:1-4 relationship to elders.
7. What should a congregation do if it doesn't have elders?
8. Why don't some preachers preach the word?
9. Do you demand "sound doctrine?"
10. How much time should the preacher be expected to study?
11. Why don't some brethren like sound preaching?
12. What are some of the subjects that are unpopular for the preacher to discuss?
13. Why do many congregations neglect discipline?
14. Is discipline just "marking a name of the roll book?"
15. When was the last time your congregation withdrew from someone?
16. Why should withdrawing be the last step?
17. Discuss the procedure for withdrawing.
18. Why is it important that each member know that he is important?
19. How can we go about helping each member feel important?
20. Discuss I Corinthians 12:12-31.
21. Do you feel important?
22. Will you make it your personal goal to encourage someone this week?
23. Why must Christ be the heart of our plans and programs?
24. Share some nominal drawing powers you have heard of, or know about, etc.
25. Do you believe that Christ is sufficient? Why?

LESSON ELEVEN
Leaders And Church Growth (II)

INTRODUCTION

In this lesson we want to look at some additional factors essential to church growth.

"Unless you try to do something beyond what you have already mastered, you (or the church) will never grow."

"God never puts any man (or church) in a place too small to grow."

Good leadership is constantly planning, praying and working for good, solid church growth. Their growth program will include some of the following ingredients:

First, every congregation must have a strong educational program. This program must provide good, sound classes and learning opportunities for *all* ages. In order to plan and carry out such a program it is necessary for leaders to have a sound, basic concept of religious education. This philosophy will stem from their understanding of the aims and objectives of religious education. If they have a clear understanding of the end goal of Christian education, their concept of education will, also, be clear.

Through the years the word *education* has been given various definitions. A good definition is essential to proper understanding of religious education on the congregational level.

The word *education* comes from the Latin *educere,* which is of the third conjugation, and means "to lead out." Thus, education may be thought of as the process of drawing out the inherent abilities in a person and developing them. As we look a little closer, however, we learn that *educere* is from the first conjugation and the form is *educare.* This term differs and means "to nourish or nurture." This term conveys the idea of supplying for or sustenance rather than drawing out. This is why a proper concept of education requires both ideas: an in-filling and a drawing out. Therefore, our educational process within the church must contain impression and expression — nourishing and exercising. James described this when he wrote, "But be ye doers of the word, and not hearers only, deceiving your own selves" (James 1:22).

In summary a good educational program will: (a) impart knowledge; (b) develop inherent abilities; (c) motivate to godly living; (d) produce carry over activities; (e) produce spiritual growth; (f) provides inspiration; (g) help develop self-control; (h) involve participation; (i) center in God's word; (j) be on each student's level; (k) demand a good curriculum; (l) use innovations in teaching; (m) require prepared teachers; (n) require adequate facilities; (o) motivate to evangelism and other good works, etc.

A good educational program is a must for the future of the local church. Leaders would do well to learn a lesson from the Jews who have always placed a great emphasis on education as a means of promoting their religion. In fact, Hosea stated that one of the reasons for the Jews going into captivity was because of a "lack of knowledge" (Cf. Hosea 4:6-8). Leaders, therefore, must diligently work to organize, promote and enlarge the educational program for maximum efficiency and outreach. An educated church is a growing church.

Second, in order to insure church growth a good work program must be organized and maintained. This program must be extensive and comprehensive enough to challenge the abilities and interests of each member of the congregation. The programs must be clearly stated along with the abilities needed to carry them out. Every child of God must know the joy of working in the Master's service; and work wrought out in activities which bless others produces joy in the heart of the one who does it.

WORK FOR CHRIST
1. The *field* is large (Matthew 13:38).
2. The *need* is great (John 4:35).
3. The *time* is now (Galatians 1:10).
4. The *call* is urgent (Matthew 20:6).
5. The *work* is varied (I Corinthians 12:12).
6. The *partner* is almighty (II Corinthians 6:1).
7. The *means* are provided (Luke 19:15).

Third, preachers must stay. This will insure stability in the preaching ministry of the congregation. Check any congregation that is accomplishing great things in the Lord's service and you will, as a general rule, find that the local preacher has been with the church for a number of years. We cannot change preachers every 2, 3 or 4 years and expect to produce strong preachers, programs, and congregations. This is why a congregation should be very careful in selecting a man to work with them as an evangelist. In many cases, however, this has not been the case.

Somewhere, at sometime, no one really knows when, a system was inaugurated within the Lord's church of using the pulpit to

LEADERS AND CHURCH GROWTH (II)

try out preachers. Traditionally this practice has been used as one of the main criterions for determining a preacher's ability to do an effective work with a local congregation. The idea seems to be that if he is a good sermonizer, he must also be a good evangelist. This may or may not be true. I know some very effective workers for the Lord who have never been rated highly (by the standards of men) as pulpiteers, and thus their needed talents on several occasions have been rejected by congregations because they were not as good as brother Doe was in the pulpit. I personally believe, while I am not opposed to them, that try out sermons have their limitations in determining a man's ability to do the work of an evangelist with a local congregation.

Really, what can you know about a man's ability to do local work by listening to him preach one or two sermons? Being a good man in the pulpit is one thing; doing the work of an evangelist is another. Most preachers have at least two sermons they can deliver well, and especially so, if a "job" depends upon it. This is not to question the sincerity, integrity, motives, or ability of any congregation or preacher who uses such an arrangement; it has worked well in many cases. On the other hand, it has caused many problems for the congregation and the preacher who knew very little about each other. This is especially true when they have different ideas about what constitutes the work of an evangelist. Misunderstandings of this nature, and many others, have led to discontentment, strife, and division within churches. This is true for small congregations without elders on frequent occasions, and has even destroyed some completely. They become so enthusiastic about the possibility of brother X working with them that they rush into securing his services on the basis of his pulpit ability. After a few months they find out what a tragic mistake they have made, as they sit in despair trying to put the pieces back together again.

Many ingredients go into making a preacher effective in local work. Most of these cannot be ascertained from a try out sermon. A try out sermon will not reveal the evangelist to be an example in ALL things (Cf. II Timothy 4:12). It is one thing to appear good in a pulpit, and quite another to live a consistent life. The try out sermon will not reveal the preacher's ability to patiently set things in order (Cf. Titus 1:5). The try out sermon will not reveal if the preacher is convinced that his task is to be out where the lost are on a daily basis (Mark 16:15, 16; Acts 20:20). Neither is it possible to know a preacher's past from a try out sermon.

Jesus makes it clear that we can know a man by his fruits (Matthew 7:20; 3:8). If the preacher is a "hobbiest" it will not come out in the try out sermon. How tragic to find this out too late. The selecting of a preacher by a congregation is not an easy task. The possibility of mistakes will always exist. This is true for the preacher as well as the congregation. But many of the problems could be eliminated if elderships and congregational leadership would be a little more cautious in selecting a preacher. Some congregations use all or a combination of the following things to help them reach a decision in selecting a preacher: (a) they make a thorough check of his last work, including his financial standing with local businesses; (b) they invite him to come for a week of gospel meetings. This will give a greater opportunity for the congregation to see the preacher do evangelistic work among the lost of the community. It will also give many of the members an opportunity to have him into their homes. This will help them to get to know one another better. Some congregations also invite the preacher to bring his family if it is at all possible; (c) some congregations ask the preacher to present lessons on special subjects for advanced classes. This helps to determine the preacher's study habits, as well as his overall knowledge of the Bible and his ability to teach on an advanced level; (d) there is also an increasing practice of elderships going to the congregation where the preacher is presently working. They are able to observe him during various preaching and teaching situations as he normally conducts himself; (e) elderships usually have several discussion sessions with a preacher before they secure his services. In these sessions they discuss the Lord's work, doctrinal issues, matters of opinions, etc. If there is a clash, it may be worked out. But if it is not worked out, this may prevent the preacher from coming to work with the congregation, and thus prevent even greater problems later. Also, the preacher may learn some things about the congregation which may change his mind about wanting to work with them; (f) the congregation makes a careful study of the work and qualifications of an evangelist before they launch into the selection of a preacher. We do this for elders, why not for preachers too? Select a good preacher and keep him. This will help the church to grow in all areas. Preachers need to stay with a congregation and stop running every time a problem comes up. After all, their mission is to set things in order. If a tree is transplanted each year it will not produce fruit. The same is true of preachers!

LEADERS AND CHURCH GROWTH (II)

Fourth, there must be clear and frequent communications. It is essential that all members and leaders communicate. An uninformed congregation is an unprepared congregation. Good communication is characterized by mutual trust, cooperation and understanding. Leaders must keep all avenues of communications open to insure church growth.

Fifth, do not worry about external problems or conditions. These do not (or should not) determine growth. They should be turned into opportunities for accelerating growth, but not detering it. Good leadership views every problem as an opportunity. With God's help all things are possible.

Sixth, the congregation must be informed of all good works. Familiarity with brotherhood works will encourage and excite the local congregation. Many of these works (churches) send out newsletters, etc., upon request. Most of these are free. For example *World Radio News* is sent free to over 225,000 persons. This paper informs about world mission work and other good works. Another way of informing the congregation is to have guest speakers from time to time present their works. Sad to say, some congregations have a "closed door" policy toward visiting missionaries or others who want to speak on behalf of a good work. Even though you may not be able to give financial assistance to them, you can, however, listen to them speak. It will be a blessing. Every leader would do well to ponder the following words of the apostle John:

"Beloved, thou doest faithfully whatsoever thou doest to the brethren, and to strangers; which have borne witness of thy charity before the church: whom if thou bring forward on their journey after a godly sort, thou shalt do well: Because that for his name's sake they went forth, taking nothing of the Gentiles. We therefore ought to receive such, that we might be fellow-helpers to the truth" (III John 1:5-8.

Another good way of informing the congregation is by having a world mission forum or workshop. This will do wonders for the local spirit of evangelism.

Seventh, stewardship must be fully understood and stressed. Each member must know his responsibility as a "manager" of time, abilities and finances. Especially in the area of finances do we have a need to educate. It takes planned, purposeful, sacrificial giving to move the church forward. "Token" offerings will not get the job done. Members must be taught to give as they are prospered (II Corinthians 8, 9); and in this day and time this is quite frequently. A good budget must be prepared and presented to the congregation. It must be a realistic budget while at the same time large enough to challenge the stewardship of each member. It must also be stressed that the Lord's money must be spent. The church is not in the banking (savings) business.

Eighth, special emphasis must be given to edification. The spirituality of each member must be constantly before the leadership. Special goals must be set, and ways of determining if they have been met, must be available for every member. It is not enough to say "our goal is for every member to grow spiritually", we must have specific ways of finding out if the members are growing. This takes us back to the key of communications.

Ninth, faith must motivate and determine every move. We must "walk by faith and not by sight." Our faith must be larger than our own strength and the balance on our check book. We must "launch out into the deep." Trust God, He will provide. With His help we CAN do all things.

Tenth, leaders must be constantly trained. This includes those who are presently leading as well as those who are preparing to lead. Leadership must "reproduce" itself. If it does not it will become extinct. Tomorrow's leaders must be trained and prepared today. The future of church growth depends upon this important factor.

Eleventh, an atmosphere of reverence must prevail in worship services. Reverence must characterize our prayers, devotion, fellowship, singing and assembling together. This will require teaching and planning. Each member should prepare himself to come and worship with saints. And above all, we should be careful to maintain quietness during services.

Twelfth, a good Bible school program must be maintained. This is an arm of the educational program of the church that deserves some special attention. A few years ago I read the following information that places proper emphasis upon the Bible school.

SEVEN REASONS FOR GOING TO BIBLE SCHOOL
1. The best book is studied and taught, and I want to know it and follow it in my everyday life.
2. The best day is utilized and used, and I wish to take advantage of it too.
3. The best people are assembled and enlisted, and I desire the blessing of their fellowship and friendship.
4. The best institution is awake and at work for the Master, and

I ought to invest myself where I will do my utmost for Christ and the church.
5. The best work is being done, and I must not fail to do my part for the enlightenment, evangelization and upbuilding of my fellowman.
6. The best development is assured and attained, and I yearn to grow mentally, morally and spiritually.
7. The best equipment is supplied, adopted and inspired, and I want to be thoroughly furnished unto all good works.

(Author unknown)

Surely such an important work of the local congregation deserves our diligent work. The following principles will help in developing a good growing Bible school program: (a) we must be sold on the importance of God's word, on the importance of teaching it and reaching others to be taught; (b) enthusiastic and dedicated teachers must be consecrated to the task of teaching the Word and reaching others with the word; (c) the Bible school must be organized efficiently and effectively; (d) there must be room for growth; (e) teachers must be trained in the art of teaching and in methods of recruitment; (f) sufficient funds must be available; (g) a visitation program must be planned, inaugurated and executed; (h) a spirit of evangelism must permeate every phase of the Bible school and every teacher and worker; (i) the spirit of prayer must permeate every teacher, every class and every pupil; (j) special promotion must be given to Bible classes; (k) proper materials and subjects must be chosen for each age group; (l) a class spirit must prevail, etc.

CONCLUSION

Perhaps you have wondered by now why personal work was not discussed in detail in these two lessons on church growth. This is because the next lesson will be devoted to this most important subject.

Take the seventeen points covered in lessons ten and eleven and conduct a greater in-depth study of each one at some future date. A close adherence to them, as well as to other church growth factors, will help your congregation move forward in the Lord's service.

FOR DISCUSSION

1. Why must the church have a good educational program?
2. When does a congregation need an educational director?
3. Do we approach religious education as seriously as secular education? Why?

4. Why is it important for leaders to have a good philosophy of religious education?
5. How does religious education differ from other education?
6. In your opinion what is the major weakness in most church educational programs?
7. How would you suggest improving your congregational educational program?
8. Why is a work program necessary for church growth?
9. Do members like to work in various programs? Why?
10. Should EVERY member have something to do?
11. What is the most needed program of work in your congregation?
12. Are some programs of work stressed too much? Discuss.
13. Why should preachers stay with a congregation for many years?
14. What is the longest period you have heard of a preacher staying with one congregation?
15. Why do most congregations use the try out method for selecting a preacher?
16. When should a preacher leave a congregation?
17. How is the BEST way of going about selecting a new preacher?
18. Have you ever studied the work and qualifications of an evangelist?
19. Why does a congregation need a preacher?
20. To what extent do external conditions determine growth?
21. Why is communications important?
22. Why should congregations be informed about all good works?
23. How do you feel about letting missionaries come and speak to the congregation?
24. What is your understanding of III John 1:5-8?
25. Why is giving a touchy subject in many congregations?
26. How much should a Christian give to the local church?
27. Why is faith essential to church growth?
28. Why do we walk by sight?
29. Why should a congregation constantly be training leaders?
30. Why are some worship services not conducive to reverence?
31. Why is a good Bible school program important?
32. What is the major need of your Bible school program?
33. List any other major points relative to church growth not covered in lessons ten and eleven.

LESSON TWELVE
Leaders And Evangelism

INTRODUCTION

Before His ascension to heaven, Jesus said, "Go ye into all the world and preach the gospel to every creature. He that believeth and is baptized shall be saved, he that believeth not shall be damned" (Mark 16:15, 16). Most Christians can quote these verses from memory because the great commission is one of the most familiar teachings of Jesus. Yet, it is one of the most neglected. Every child of God is implicated in world evangelism according to the above commandment. Each Christian is responsible for doing his part to evangelize the world. The early disciples of the Lord took this charge seriously and completed it within a few years (Cf. Col. 1:23). As far as I know it has not been repeated since that time. Why? Obviously EVERY child of God in our day has not taken the great commission seriously.

During the past ten to fifteen years much emphasis has been placed upon personal evangelism by churches of Christ. In fact, during the sixties we were the fastest growing religious body in America. But this is no longer true. The fire is not as bright as it once was. We have spent many hours studying personal work. We have bought books from brothers that have "set us on fire" to do personal work. Soon, however, the flame subsided and we no longer feel the urgency to seek the lost. We drift from week to week hoping the preacher will baptize someone; after all, this is what he is getting paid to do. We have purchased film strips, charts, manuals, one-shot approaches, tracts, and other aids to assist in converting the lost. Where are these aids now? In a closet or storage room collecting dust. And, yet, outside our walls the lost continue to pass by.

In recent years we have developed a new specialist within the church — the Personal Work Director. This man is trained to train and lead others in personal evangelism. This is wonderful, if we will follow him and do likewise. Yet, sad to say, in many cases this man finds himself the only doer of personal work. When will we ever wake up to the fact that we cannot hire someone to do our personal work? The false notion that only the preacher or a few talented persons should do the personal work, MUST END. Leadership, therefore, has its job cut out as it seeks to revive interest in personal evangelism. This interest must be created in the heart of EACH member. This is essential because EVANGELISM IS THE KEY TO CHURCH GROWTH. Everything else is secondary.

In this lesson we want to rekindle the fires of evangelism within the hearts of those men who lead the Lord's people. From this fire may come a spark that will kindle the hearts of those that sit on the pews.

WHY SEEK THE LOST?

Proper answers to this question should motivate us to share the gospel with every person we come in contact with. Likewise, our love for the lost should become deeper (because LOVE is the reason we seek the lost). Notice some of the following reasons why we MUST seek the lost:

(1) *Because they are in sin.* This is clearly taught in the Scriptures (Cf. Romans 3:23). The results of sin is separation from God, both in time and in eternity (Isa. 59:1, 2). Therefore, a person is dead spiritually (Ephesians 2:1; Ezekiel 18:4, 20).

(2) *Because they are without Christ.* And to be without Christ means to be *without:* (a) all spiritual blessings (Ephesians 1:3); (b) salvation (Acts 4:12); (c) hope (Colossians 1:27; Romans 8:24); (d) light; (e) strength John 15:5); (f) hope of heaven (I Peter 1:3-5); (g) life eternal (John 14:6); (h) peace (Ephesians 2:14).

(3) *Because of their destiny.* If a person dies outside of Christ the Bible tells us of their destiny. This destiny is the lake of fire (Matthew 25). It is described by the Bible as: (a) a lake of fire (Revelation 20:15); (b) a place of everlasting punishment (Matthew 25:46); (c) a place of torment (Luke 16:23); (d) a place

where people pray for help (Luke 16:24); (e) a place of darkness (Jude 13; Matthew 8:12); (f) a place where people scream for mercy (Luke 16:24); (g) a place of filthiness (Revelation 22:10, 11); (h) a place of weeping (Matthew 8:12); (i) a place of no rest (Revelation 14:11); (j) a place of damnation, world without end (Mark 3:29), etc.

The above facts causes one to shudder if he loves the souls of men. How terrible is the fate of the lost. If this awareness does not motivate us, what will? God does not leave us guessing relative to the condition of the lost — THEY ARE DAMNED by their sins! Jesus knew this very well; this is why His mission was to seek and save the lost (Luke 19:10). He did not want to see a single person go to the above described fate. His concern carried Him to a cross. Where will your concern carry you?

How about you? Do you care if those around you go head long into a devil's hell? Do you care if men without Christ are separated from Christ and God? Will you lead in seeking the lost?

We need to seek the lost because this is the only way to reach them with gospel. When we teach on a person-to-person basis it helps us to know the individual's needs. They are able to ask questions and receive answers. In person-to-person contact we are able to show our love and personal feelings for the souls of the lost. Our song must be: "Lord Lead Me To Some Soul Today".

WHAT SEEKING THE LOST WILL DO

The following material is taken from my book *Snatching Men Out Of The Fire,* pp. 128, 129 (Lambert Book House, 1974).

I. IT WILL HELP THE LOCAL CONGREGATION

    A. A church that is seeking the lost is a church that is on the move for the Master:
        1. This is the main task of the church.
        2. If sin allows the fire of evangelism to go out in the local church, it has no reason to continue.
    B. A church that is seeking the lost is a united church.
        1. There is a unity of spirit and a bond of peace (Ephesians 4:1-6).
        2. Brethren have the same care one for another.

- C. A church seeking the lost is a praying church.
    1. Acts 2:42.
    2. It will come together to pray for the lost.
- D. Helps the church to pleasing unto God as it grows.
    1. A church without its lamp lit in this dark world (I John 5:19) is running the risk of having its lampstand removed.

II. IT WILL HELP EACH CHRISTIAN
- A. Grow in grace and knowledge.
    1. You cannot go out and seek the lost without growing yourself.
    2. II Peter 1:5-7.
- B. To bear fruit for Christ.
    1. A barren belief is good for nothing.
    2. It will be cast out (Cf. John 15).
- C. To obey Christ.
    1. Every Christian is under the great commission.
    2. We must obey it!
- D. To live right.
    1. The fruit of right living is souls.
    2. We must evangelize or fossilize!
- E. To be like the Master.
    1. His mission was to seek the lost (Luke 19:10).
    2. Likewise, ours is to seek the lost.
- F. It will keep us from being foolish.
    1. He that winneth souls is wise (Proverbs 11:30).
    2. Not to win souls is foolish!

III. IT REACHES EVERY TYPE OF PERSON
- A. Every class is reached in person-to-person soul seeking:
    1. The rich and the poor.
    2. The indifferent and unconcerned.
    3. The shut-in and shut-out.

LEADERS AND EVANGELISM

   4. The sick and the well.
   5. The lukewarm and the zealous.
   6. The religious and non-religious.
   7. The educated and uneducated.
   8. All races and languages.
   9. Young, middle and old ages.
   10. Children and teenagers.
  B. Every person is approached as one sincerely seeks the lost.
   1. There is a way to reach everyone.
   2. We must pray for wisdom to know how.
   3. The thirsty need the water of life that you have to offer.

IV. IT MEETS EVERY CONDITION AND NEED
  A. Seeking the lost can be done at any time.
   1. No special day is needed.
   2. No special hour is needed.
  B. There is no special place needed in seeking the lost.
   1. It does not have to take place in a special building, etc.
   2. Anywhere the person is.
  C. There is no special worker needed for seeking the lost.
   1. Every Christian, regardless of his occupation, is a worker.
   2. E.g., the doctor, lawyer, dentist, teacher, plumber, bus driver, etc.
  D. Every talent can be used in seeking the lost.
   1. 1 talent to 100.
   2. All can tell others how to become a Christian in their own way!

Seeking the lost is important because it produces results. It can be carried on under all conditions by every child of God. It helps the local congregation *go, grow,* and *glow* for Christ. Truly Jesus was right when He said, "GO YE". What has seeking the lost done for you and the congregation where you lead and attend?

VARIED AND PERPETUAL PROGRAMS FOR SEEKING THE LOST

Each congregation, and individual, must be involved in a perpetual soul winning program. There are a variety of ways for this to be accomplished. Through the years most congregations have begun many good programs only to let them die. Sad to say, some of these dead programs have never been replaced by live ones. It is good to use a variety of programs in seeking the lost. This will keep interest and results at an all-time high. As always, planning and work are the keys to success. The following list presents only a few of the programs for seeking the lost:

I. THE YEARLY CAMPAIGN
   A. This is an organized effort to reach the lost in a gospel meeting.
   B. Some key factors to remember:
      1. It will require a dynamic speaker.
      2. It will take a group of trained campaign workers.
      3. It will require enough money to do a first class job.
      4. It will take well planned advertisement.
      5. It will require involvement of every member:
         a. Provide food, lodging, transportation for out of town workers.
         b. To work in door-to-door campaign.
      6. It will require enough tools:
         a. Film strips, projectors, tracts, maps, various printed materials.
         b. Prepare a campaign work list.
      7. It will require a well organized campaign office.
      8. The campaign must be worked on ALL year. Last minute preparation will not do.
      9. An organized follow-up program.
      10. A new convert class for the new Christians.

LEADERS AND EVANGELISM

    C. It will take several campaigns to see a great harvest:
        1. Each effort builds on the one before.
        2. Some try one time and then quit.
        3. The White's Ferry Road Church has grown in attendance from 200 in 1965 to 1,000 in 1975. A yearly campaign is responsible for much of this growth. In this year's campaign (1975) over 60 souls were baptized; and the total for the year is over 200.

II. THE SATURDAY GROUP

    A. Meet at the church building about 9:00 a.m. on Saturday for prayer and plans and then go out from about 10:00 until 12:00.
    B. Advantage of this approach:
        1. It is perpetual (52 weeks a year).
        2. All can work as they have opportunity.
    C. It requires work and organization.

III. RELIGIOUS SURVEY

    A. Prepare a good survey questionnaire.
    B. Enlist and train survey workers.
    C. Advantages of survey:
        1. Gives the congregation an opportunity to know the community.
        2. Lets the community know about the church.
        3. Will help you get into homes otherwise closed.

IV. "WE SEEK TO SERVE" PROGRAM

    A. This will let the community know that you care.
    B. Print an attractive folder advertising various services of the church:
        1. Your benevolent program.
        2. Bible study.
        3. Counseling.
        4. Transportation, etc.

V. THE 100 HOUSES APPROACH
   A. Obtain a city map.
   B. Block off 100 houses on the map:
      1. Concentrate on them until EVERYONE has been contacted.
      2. Use STAR direct mail, or your own materials.
      3. Use a phone committee.
   C. This assures complete coverage of community.
      1. If not at home keep returning.
      2. We must reach "every creature".

VI. THE CITY OR COUNTY WIDE EFFORT
   A. All area congregations cooperate in this effort.
   B. Requires long range planning.
   C. This is a good way to begin evangelization of an area.
   D. Local follow-up is very important.
   E. Preaching may be conducted in a Civic Center, etc.

VII. WEEKLY NEWSPAPER ARTICLES
   A. They must be brief and well written.
   B. Opportunity to teach masses.
   C. Vary your approach from time to time.

VIII. WEEKLY RADIO AND TV PROGRAMS
   A. A local program by local preacher or area preachers.
   B. Brotherhood programs:
      1. World Radio; Herald of Truth; The Gospel Hour.

IX. SEVERAL WEEKEND MEETINGS A YEAR
   A. Provided opportunity to invite friends.
   B. Keeps interest high.
   C. Contacts will be made.

X. A RESTORATION PROGRAM FOR MEMBERS WHO HAVE FALLEN AWAY
   A. A fallen brother is worse than a lost person (II Peter 2:20, 21).

LEADERS AND EVANGELISM

    B. We must restore the erring (Galatians 6:1, 2; James 5:19, 20).
    C. Do personal visiting prior to the meeting.

XI. A CORRESPONDENCE COURSE
    A. Sign persons up as you go from door-to-door.
    B. Place enrollment cards (boxes) in local businesses.
    C. Go to jails, nursing homes, etc., and enroll students.

XII. YOUTH GROUPS
    A. They have great talent.
    B. Use in all of the above programs.
    C. Also special soul winning effort among teens (school campus, etc.).

XIII. DISTRIBUTION OF TRACTS
    A. Select good tracts.
    B. Hand out from door-to-door.
    C. Send one in each bill you pay, etc.

XIV. BUS PROGRAM
    A. Bringing children and adults to services.
    B. Requires hard work every Saturday.

The above programs are merely suggestions. As a leader you need to get busy and promote programs that will seek and save the lost.

TAKING INVENTORY BEFORE SEEKING THE LOST

Paul said, "Examine yourselves whether ye be in the faith; prove your ownselves. Know ye not your own selves . . .". This is what we must do as leaders of the church before we go forth to seek the lost or motivate others to seek the lost. We must examine our attitude toward this great task. Is it the right attitude?

In the following examination we must be honest with ourselves and with God. This inventory is not designed to embarrass or discourage anyone. It is merely to help us get a view of our responsibilities and realize our possibilities in the great task of seeking the lost.

Yes No (Check One)

☐ ☐ 1. Do you believe men are lost outside of Christ?
☐ ☐ 2. Do you believe the lost will be cast into hell?
☐ ☐ 3. Do you believe you must teach the lost?
☐ ☐ 4. Can you hire someone to fulfill your responsibility?
☐ ☐ 5. Have you ever taught a lost person?
☐ ☐ 6. Have you ever taught and baptized a person?
_____ 7. How many persons have you taught in the last 12 months?
_____ 8. How many persons have you baptized during the past 12 months or had a part in helping to become a Christian?
☐ ☐ 9. Do you know what a person must believe to be saved?
☐ ☐ 10. Do you know what a person must do in order to be saved?
☐ ☐ 11. Can you find the above (9, 10) information in your Bible?
☐ ☐ 12. Do you have the above information memorized?
☐ ☐ 13. Will you teach someone the gospel this month? If you answered yes, write the name on this line _____.
☐ ☐ 14. Do you need to repent of neglecting soul winning?
☐ ☐ 15. Does your congregation have an organized personal evangelism program?
☐ ☐ 16. Is personal work essential to church growth?
☐ ☐ 17. Should leaders do personal work?
☐ ☐ 18. Have you had a study in personal work methods?
☐ ☐ 19. Do you have the ability to teach a lost person the gospel?
☐ ☐ 20. Do you have the ability to knock on a person's door?

LEADERS AND EVANGELISM

Yes No (Check One)

☐ ☐ 21. Do you have the ability to pass out tracts?

☐ ☐ 22. Do you think you will be lost if you don't teach the lost?

☐ ☐ 23. Do you love the lost?

☐ ☐ 24. Do you try to excuse yourself by saying, "I am too busy to do personal work?

☐ ☐ 25. Do you think you need more training?

☐ ☐ 26. Do you pray for the lost daily?

☐ ☐ 27. With God's help will you seek the lost?

☐ ☐ 28. Are you ashamed of the gospel of Christ?

☐ ☐ 29. Can you go with someone else to teach the lost?

☐ ☐ 30. Will you study your Bible for personal work purposes?

☐ ☐ 31. Do you know a lost person? Write down his name:

_____

☐ ☐ 32. Do you have a good influence on a lost person?

☐ ☐ 33. Have you ever talked to a person on your job about the gospel?

☐ ☐ 34. Will you talk to someone on the job about the gospel?

☐ ☐ 35. Are you ready to lead others in soul winning?

CONCLUSION

In closing I call your attention to the words of Norman Lewis, "To evangelize the world is the most significant business on earth. 'Why is that' you ask. Because of its motive." Thus, because Christ means more to us than the very air we breath, we love the lost and will seek them until the end. A church that evangelizes is a church that is growing and pleasing unto God. As God's leader, be out in front looking for the lost. Someone will follow you!

LESSON THIRTEEN
Leaders And Business Meetings

INTRODUCTION

Webster defines *meeting* as, "a coming together of persons or things." For leadership to function properly meetings must occur. Most of the things discussed in this book necessitate meetings for implementation to occur. There are many kinds of meetings that leaders will be involved in. Some of these are: (1) elders meetings; (2) deacons meetings; (3) teachers meetings; (4) committee meetings; (5) elders meeting with various groups, e.g., ladies, men, teens, etc.; (6) meetings of special groups, e.g., senior citizens, teens, etc.; (7) staff meetings, e.g., secretary, janitor, etc.; (8) general business meetings. It is especially to this last one that we want to direct our attention. From the business meeting comes most of the plans and goals for church growth. As a rule, the other meetings are preparatory for the general business meeting, or the results of the business meeting.

PROBLEMS

Most preachers, elders, deacons, and concerned Christian leaders have felt the frustration of trying to get other men within the congregation to attend business meetings. Most of us have tried to encourage other men to attend, only to hear replies such as: "Oh, you don't need me"; "I don't have the time"; "it is already cut and dry"; "they never discuss anything important"; "I don't like to argue"; "they meet too often"; "I don't like business meetings", etc. Certainly we would be amiss if we didn't realize the validity of some of these statements. Our purpose, however, is not to examine their validity, but try to provide incentives and encouragements to all men of the congregation to attend called (emergency or special) or regular business meetings of the local church. Leadership, therefore, must take every precaution to insure communications in this very important field.

WHAT IS A BUSINESS MEETING?

In a word, it is an expedient. To this, however, additional remarks need to be addressed. It is a time to prayerfully consider the many areas of work carried on by the local congregation. Things just don't happen! It takes vision, planning, work, discussion, and many other things to move the local church forward in the Lord's work. A good, well organized business meeting will help produce short and long range plans that will keep the church growing for years to come. Good leadership knows this and acts accordingly.

REASONS FOR ATTENDING

First, because you are an important member of the church. Paul points this out in I Corinthians 12:13-27. The body, if it is to properly function, must have the strength and activity of each member. If one member fails to function, the whole body suffers. Likewise, if some men don't show up at business meetings, the church suffers. You are needed!

Second, because the business to be discussed is the greatest in the world — the Lord's business! In the everyday business world, meetings are held by the thousands to discuss temporal or material things. Many men will travel great distances, go without sleep, etc., to attend such meetings. Yet, sad to say, some of these same men will not attend a church business meeting. We must place the kingdom first (Cf. Matthew 6:33). The salvation of souls, edification of the body, and doing good unto all men, are some important reasons for attending business meetings. In fact, nothing is more important.

Third, because you let the Lord and others know that you care. Like it or not, many brethren view those who do not attend business meetings as unconcerned about the Lord's work, especially in the local situation. It's hard to convince someone you care about the church when you don't support its programs, or attend its meetings. We must let our lights shine (Cf. Matthew 6:13-16). We must be an example of a believer in ALL things (Cf. I Timothy 4:12). Remember these words, "A good example is worth a thousand sermons."

Fourth, because of the fellowship. Business meetings provide a wonderful opportunity for the men of the church to be together in prayer, song, discussion, and a general sharing of brotherly love as they discuss the greatest work in the world. The church becomes stronger and more united as the members associate one with another. Jesus said, "By this shall all men know that ye are my disciples, if ye have love one to another" (John 13:35). Unity among brethren is pleasant in God's sight (Cf. Psalm 133:1-3; Ephesians 4:1-5).

Fifth, because you have a chance to be heard. We hear a lot today about what is wrong with the church. Some of those doing the complaining won't lift a finger to do anything about it, or attend business meetings so they can speak out and offer their suggestions and advice in constructive ways to help eliminate these problems. It is still true that *action* speaks louder than words. The business meeting is where the action is — attend them if you want to be heard. Remember the power of leaven!

Sixth, because it will encourage others. We all need encourment from time to time. Whether the business meeting is called by the elders, or one conducted by men in a congregation without elders, it is discouraging to see only a few show up for a meeting to discuss the local work. Your presence will encourage the elders, deacons, preacher, and other brethren who attend.

Seventh, because you have a responsibility. As a child of God, and a member of Christ's church, you have a responsibility to see that the gospel is preached (Mark 16:15, 16); the poor are helped (James 1:27); and to bring glory to God in the church (Ephesians 3:21). It is not possible for anyone else to fulfill your responsibility in the local church.

It is true that many business meetings have been no more than wrangling sessions, or an hour spent on which color to paint a classroom. This does not mean, however, that we should forsake these meetings. On the contrary, we must put a lot of prayer, planning and work into them to insure their success. A good rule is: BUSINESS MEETINGS ARE FOR BUSINESS (the Lord's business). Therefore, let's handle them as wise stewards and support them with our presence. To do so, is a sign of good leadership.

SOME GUIDELINES

God has ordained that things in His church be done "decently and in order" (I Corinthians 14:40). This is a must for good business

LEADERS AND BUSINESS MEETINGS

meetings. Good procedure does not just happen, it must be planned and worked on before it can become a reality. The following guidelines will insure order:

(1) Select a person to serve as chairman of the meeting. It is his responsibility to call the meeting to order and maintain order during the meeting. The chairman should be familiar with *Roberts Rules Of Order* (it may be purchased at any bookstore).

(2) There must be a prepared agenda. This will keep the meeting on a specific course, as well as preventing it from becoming a discussion of trivial matters. Prepare your agenda and stick to it.

(3) The areas discussed should pertain to the purpose and agenda of the meeting. A deacons' meeting, for example, will discuss work particular to deacons.

(4) Each man, or committee should have an opportunity to report, or state opinions, suggestions, etc. The chairman will be careful to keep the meeting moving on the subject at hand.

(5) Cover one subject at a time. Trying to cover several at one time will only confuse.

(6) Accurate minutes of the meeting should be kept. This is a must for safety as well as IRS regulations.

(7) Confidential discussions in meetings should be kept confidential. This does not mean to go straight home and tell your wife or anyone else. This has done much harm within the Lord's church through the years. Be careful!

(8) Be sure that all areas, if possible, are guided by Scripture. Do not take authority you do not have. On one occasion I heard of a congregation voting on whether or not a person of another race could attend their congregation. They do not have this right, if the Scriptures are followed. Be careful, therefore, of majority or minority rule. God's word rules!

(9) They must not be cut and dried before the meeting starts. Sometimes, unfortunately, leaders have caucused prior to the official meeting and determined what actions should be taken or a particular course that will be followed. Such politicing is wrong. Do not gather "votes" before the meeting.

(10) As a general rule all meetings should be announced well enough in advance so as to permit enough time for everyone to make plans to attend. Do not, if possible, spring them at the last minute.

(11) Set a time limit for the meeting. There may be a rare exception when you will need to go over, but as a general rule respect the alloted time.

(12) Open every meeting with a prayer. This is God's business and we must ask Him for wisdom as we conduct it.

(13) Each person should pay close attention to all discussions in the meeting. This will aid understanding, as well as eliminating unnecessary questions. From time to time, however, it will be necessary to ask questions. Be sure you have thought through your question before you ask it.

(14) Do not get bogged down. This happens sometimes in insignificant areas, such as what size should the new light bulbs be, or when should be drain the baptistry, etc.

(15) Each person should give careful prayer and thought to what he brings up in a meeting. (The exception would be if the meeting is a brainstorming session). Don't talk just for the sake of talking.

SPECIAL MEETINGS

Before closing this lesson on business meetings, a special word is in order for special meetings. By this I mean a special time and place for conducting a business meeting or an information meeting. These are the meetings that take place at other places rather than at the church building. Some of these are:

(1) The men's retreat. This type of meeting may be conducted on the weekend or on a Saturday, or even on a Friday night. During the years that I have been working with the White's Ferry Road congregation one of the highlights of the year is a year-end retreat with all of the men of the congregation. This is conducted in December on a Friday evening. At this appointed time the men come together at a youth camp just a few miles from the church building and share a "pot luck" supper. After this each man is given a printed booklet with a resume of the past year's accomplishments by the congregation. (This year the booklet contained 28 pages on all phases of our work). From this time on, the "spiritual feast" and challenges begin. This year approximately 300 men sat on the edge of their seats and shared in the four hour program prepared by the elders of the church. Below I have included a copy of the program to illustrate an approach to a retreat program:

WHITE'S FERRY ROAD MEN'S RETREAT
December 12, 1975
"Stretching Forward"

PROGRAM

6:30-6:45	Registration (name tags, booklets, etc.)	
6:45-7:45	Supper	
7:45-8:00	Singspiration	
8:00-8:10	"Stretching Forward"	J. J. Turner
8:10-9:00	Reflections — "What We Have Done!"	
	Joy Bus Program	Randall Dunagan
	Puppet Program	J. R. Baker
	Child Care	Jim Moran
	Foreign Missions	Jim Moran
	Local Evangelism	Bill Smith
	Benevolence	Buster Keeton
	Advanced Bible Classes	Blaine Adkins
	Silver Eagle Bus Work	Ben Cumnock
	Van bus work	Larry Earwood
	"Let The Bible Speak" TV program	Jerry Madden
9:00-9:10	STRETCH	
9:10-10:00	Challenge — "WHAT MUST I DO!"	
	Building program	Norm Rhodes
	AMEN program	Don Yelton
	Bible School program	Dub Deloach
	School of Biblical Studies	Carl Allison
	World Radio	Hal Frazier
	Personal Evangelism	Perry Smith
	Jolly Sixties	Tony Hawk
10:00-10:20	Questions and Answers	Alton Howard (elder)
10:20-10:35	Devotional	John Lucas
	Dismissal prayer	Guy Elliott

Needless to say everyone left this retreat feeling inspired, informed and motivated to do more in the Lord's work during the coming year. I might also add that the congregation has a mid-year retreat which serves as a checkup point and additional source of encouragement and motivation. Your congregation would greatly benefit from such sessions. Be sure to include them in this year's plans.

(2) The breakfast meeting. This, as the name implies, takes place in the morning. Any morning of the week is okay. This type of meeting is usually limited to one or two points of business. On some occasions it is strictly for fellowship and prayer. There is something dynamic about getting together early in the morning and discussing the Lord's work. Try it and see.

CONCLUSION

Leaders recognize the need for good communications within the church membership. Business meetings, and other meetings, are major avenues through which communications occur. Therefore, plan them wisely and prayerfully. By so doing you will lead the church of the Lord in your location to victory. May God help you as you remember the words of Paul:

"Therefore, my beloved brethren, be ye steadfast, unmoveable, always abounding in the work of the Lord, forasmuch as ye know that your labour is not in vain in the Lord" (I Corinthians 15:58).

FOR DISCUSSION

1. Why are business meetings essential to church growth?
2. Why do some men stay away from business meetings?
3. List other types of meetings not mentioned in the lesson.
4. In what areas do most business meetings need improvement?
5. Discuss the worst business meeting you have ever been in (be careful).
6. Discuss the best business meeting you have ever been in.
7. Why should a man attend business meetings? Give some additional ones.
8. Why should confidential business be kept confidential?
9. Does your congregation keep accurate minutes of all business meetings?

LEADERS AND BUSINESS MEETINGS

10. Is it a good practice to publish for the membership the important points in the business meeting? Why?
11. How about tape recording business meetings? Discuss.
12. How is an easy way to get off the subject in a meeting?
13. Are your congregational business meetings well attended?
14. Formulate a plan to get every man to your next business meeting.
15. Should majority rule? Discuss.
16. How do you feel about "politicing" before a business meeting?
17. Does your congregation conduct an annual retreat?
18. What is the date of your next retreat?_____
19. Why does "getting away" help?
20. Discuss the benefits of a breakfast for the men.
21. Present some other "special" meeting opportunities.
22. What do you plan to do in the coming year to promote business meetings?
23. Do you have a copy of *Roberts Rules Of Order?* Will you buy one?
24. When is your next business meeting?_____
25. Are all men informed well in advance of the meeting?

Appendix

125 "DO'S" AND "DON'TS" FOR LEADERS

1. Don't leave God out of your plans.
2. Don't neglect daily prayer.
3. Don't procrastinate.
4. Do unto others as you would have them do unto you.
5. Don't let discouragement turn into defeat.
6. Do something about your bad habit(s) each day.
7. Don't be negative.
8. Do something each day toward reaching your goal.
9. Don't be content with past success.
10. Do it differently if possible.
11. Don't be late for an appointment.
12. Don't worry about tomorrow.
13. Do the best job possible.
14. Don't underestimate the abilities of others.
15. Don't belittle people.
16. Don't neglect record keeping.
17. Don't waste time on unimportant details.
18. Don't go when you can call.
19. Don't neglect your goals.
20. Don't worry about what might have been.
21. Do your part to insure success.
22. Don't neglect Bible study.
23. Don't stop learning and growing in knowledge.
24. Don't give up when the going gets rough.
25. Do something for relaxation weekly.
26. Don't neglect your health.
27. Don't worry about people disagreeing with you.
28. Don't waste your time.
29. Don't make excuses.
30. Do your priorities first.
31. Don't forget to smile.
32. Do a good deed as often as possible.
33. Don't turn down new ideas too quickly.
34. Do God's will with diligence.
35. Do something for/with your family.
36. Do a day's work for a day's pay.
37. Don't neglect your obligations.
38. Don't forget to think before you speak.
39. Don't neglect your appearance.
40. Do the Lord's work with joy.
41. Don't find fault.
42. Don't be afraid to stand for your convictions.
43. Don't forget to write it down.
44. Do a thorough job of preparation.
45. Don't forget to make a checklist.
46. Don't be afraid to say NO

APPENDIX

47. Don't waste time on the phone.
48. Don't overlook the obvious.
49. Do expect the unexpected.
50. Don't put off making decisions.
51. Don't get bogged down in "busywork".
52. Don't be afraid to change.
53. Don't worry about making a mistake.
54. Don't jump to conclusions.
55. Do your best to stay alert.
56. Don't forget to keep an up-to-date calendar.
57. Do hard things FIRST.
58. Do a thorough job of examining yourself.
59. Don't neglect your sleep and rest.
60. Do ask questions.
61. Do keep a time schedule.
62. Don't neglect "Thank you".
63. Don't remain status quo.
64. Don't neglect the facts.
65. Don't forget to delegate.
66. Don't forget alternatives.
67. Don't forget to learn from failures.
68. Don't watch too much TV.
69. Don't be afraid to say, "I was wrong".
70. Do it better the second time, etc.
71. Don't neglect additional training.
72. Don't live in the past.
73. Don't run from problems.
74. Do think BIG.
75. Don't forget you are not alone.
76. Don't be a slave to traditions.
77. Don't be afraid to be "original".
78. Do today's work today.
79. Don't forget to "dream".
80. Don't lose your temper.
81. Do forgive others.
82. Don't lose your enthusiasm.
83. Don't take people for granted.
84. Do your "homework".
85. Don't forget to walk by faith.
86. Don't forget to be a gentleman.
87. Do dynamic things for the cause of Christ.
88. Do accept challenges.
89. Don't take your problems to bed with you.
90. Don't gossip.
91. Don't let your plans die.
92. Don't pass the buck.
93. Do try harder.
94. Don't overdo a good thing.

APPENDIX

95. Don't leave things to chance.
96. Do something for a friend.
97. Don't forget to be friendly.
98. Don't let pride destroy you.
99. Do something for an enemy.
100. Don't fail to grow in love and patience.
101. Do what you say you will do.
102. Don't always take the line of least resistance.
103. Don't settle for mediocrity.
104. Do something to improve your initiative.
105. Don't lose your ambition.
106. Do the "impossible" with God's help.
107. Don't linger on the horizon — move on!
108. Do things to insure good communications.
109. Do away with pessimism.
110. Don't mingle with failure.
111. Don't lose sight of your possibilities.
112. Don't be afraid to sacrifice for what you want.
113. Do something for self-improvement.
114. Don't let your environment discourage you.
115. Do things that arouse the BEST in others.
116. Don't chase shadows.
117. Don't compromise the truth.
118. Don't expect success without work.
119. Do away with selfishness.
120. Don't convince yourself that you are too old.
121. Don't become a victim of laziness.
122. Don't be a respecter of persons.
123. Don't lose your aspiration.
124. Don't major in minors.
125. Do all things for the glory of God.